MW01179071

Rejoice Always

52 Lessons on Joy

by
Father Clair Watrin

Arranged and Edited
By
Alice Murray

My goal for life and my message to all "Rejoice always, pray constantly and give thanks in all situations, for this is the will of God for you in Christ Jesus." 1Thessalonians 5:16

TRYING TO LIVE THIS SCRIPTURE HAS CHANGED MY WHOLE LIFE. I send it to you with my love and prayers. Fr. Clair

Copyright 2020

Watrin, Clair; Author
Murray, Alice; Editor

Rejoice Always, 52 Lessons on Joy by Father Clair Watrin

Cover design by Kate Beaton

ISBN
(softcover) 978-1-6568-3488-1

1.Christianity 2. Religion 3. Inspirational

Imprint Independently Published

All rights reserved. No part of this publication may be reproduced, stored in a retrieval system, or transmitted in any form, or by any means, electronic, mechanical, photocopying, recording or otherwise without the written permission of the editor.

murralice@gmail.com

Dedication

I dedicate my work on this book to
Janet Small
And
Real Lamontagne
You have shown me the way of angels.

Alice Murray

Contents

Forward

I am a cradle Catholic. Baptized into the faith and taught from an early age that Jesus loves me. Through my day to day existence, and many trials, I was aware that He was there, giving me the strength to get through the hard times, although for me it always seemed more of an academic belief rather than a heartfelt one.

In early 2012, my family was facing a difficult situation. Our daughter and son-in-law were expecting their third child, and we had gotten the incredible news that she was carrying twins, with the caveat that the twins were in grave danger due to a medical condition.

In February, my friend invited us to a "Live-In Retreat." I didn't know what it was about, but thought maybe it would help us in praying for our twin grandsons. When we walked into the retreat, there was a huge poster that covered an entire wall of the room which simply read, "Expect a Miracle."

That weekend two miracles happened. First, the medical condition threatening our twin grandsons vanished. They are now healthy, happy seven-year-olds. Secondly, I experienced first hand the love of Jesus through the speakers and people putting on the retreat. It completely transformed my heart and my life. Love and joy had replaced all the sadness, wounds, and hurt in my heart from past trials. I developed a real thirst to know Jesus better and joined a Bible study. I longed to serve Jesus and joined the Live-In movement on their Core team to put on future retreats. And then that Easter, I met Father Clair.

Father Clair Watrin is a humble and joy-filled priest who was born and raised in Alberta and had been a priest for over 50 years at that point. He came to our parish to teach the Lenten Mission, from his post at the Way of Holiness Retreat Center in Hinton, Alberta. Father Clair was responsible for creating the Live-In Retreat movement in 1973 in Lethbridge, and it had spread through Western Canada, Nova Scotia, and Saint Lucia.

His Lenten Mission was full of his wit, wisdom, and childlike faith and touched my heart greatly. After the mission, I approached him to thank him for creating the Live-In and tell him of the miracles it had manifested in my life but could get out only tears of gratitude and no words. He patted my shoulder, gave me a beautiful smile, and whispered to me, "Give all the glory to God."

Father Clair has an email blog with hundreds of followers that he continues to write, even in retirement. He asked me one day if I could put some of his work together in a book. I said with the help and guidance of God, I would certainly try. I went through hundreds of Father Clair's blogs and pulled out, arranged, and edited some of his writings on suffering, forgiveness, being overwhelmed, and living in the 'now' moment. The theme of all of his blogs is to seek God, where God is there is joy.

His writings are often autobiographical, sometimes humourous, and always inspiring. For years his sign off on his blog has been the verse from 1Thesselonians 5:16 "Rejoice always, pray constantly, give thanks in all situations, for this is God's will for you in Christ Jesus." This is Father Clair's mantra, which he tries to live every day and encourages us all to do the same. It seemed the best title for the book.

It blesses me significantly knowing Father Clair, reading his reflections, and working on his book, and I hope it will bless all who read it and help you to find more joy in your life.

Your Sister in Christ
Alice Murray

Introduction

'Amazing Grace' is the sentiment that overwhelms me when I think of my years as a priest. What made me decide to become a priest is the thought of what I would wish I had done at the hour of my death. I thought that when I face my judgment, I would want to have lived a life of service to God and others, and God in his mercy has given me this through the Basilians. I was ordained as a Catholic priest in the congregation of Saint Basil in 1959. I was in ministry from 1949 to 2016. Over my more than 60 years in ministry, I've served the Lord in many ways. I taught secondary school for 15 years; I was a chaplain at the University of Lethbridge for four years; I organized youth retreats for many years and have often preached parish missions. I was in St Lucia doing missionary work for 16 years.

As a Basilian I have been stationed in Sudbury, Saskatoon, Lethbridge, Windsor, and St. Lucia. In each one of these places God has blessed me and helped me to keep growing in faith and love. God was so good to me as I always enjoyed my life in each place that I lived. I am so grateful to God and the Basilians. I have had trials and temptations, but God in His mercy and love has brought good and healing out of it all.

I brought a retreat program for students called 'The Search' to Canada in 1970 and started an adult retreat movement called Live-In in 1973. This retreat movement spread all across Western Canada and into Nova Scotia and St. Lucia. The Live-In has touched thousands of lives profoundly. I had no idea that God would use it this powerfully.

What great love He has. God likes to choose the poor weak ones like me to do His work because we could do nothing by ourselves, and we know for sure it is all the mercy and work of God and give Him all of the glory and thanks. All I did was to stretch His mercy and patience when I was not the instrument he called me to be.

In the final six years of my ministry, I had a significant role in the direction and growth of a retreat centre called 'The Way of Holiness' in Hinton, Alberta. During my time at Hinton, I was the retreat preacher at many parish Lenten missions across western Canada. The main gift that God gave me in all of these ministries was to teach and to preach. I am most grateful that God used me in these ministries of evangelizing.

I was in western Canada for thirty years. Everything at the retreat centre was going great, and I was busy evangelizing and had made many commitments for the next year to preach retreats. However, I received a letter that I was to transfer to Toronto for retirement. I had to leave all of those I knew and loved; my only sister, my closest friends, and family. This was like dying. It was death to all that I love. I had all sorts of plans and commitments for retreats and parish missions and a conference on Vancouver Island. Then suddenly, I was told that I had to go to Toronto to the retirement home, and there I would not preach or do any ministry. I had four weeks to report there.

After all of the years with my heart in ministry, it was tough not to be able to do any of the things that I treasured and enjoyed. I had to leave not only those I loved but also the work I loved. The letter made me feel very angry and upset. I did not want to accept this plan. However, God, in His mercy, showed me that I have a vow of obedience. In my flesh, I did not want to accept this. It was a difficult struggle, and I needed the grace of God to conquer my self-will and rebellion.

It was tempting to be angry and complain and tell everyone it was unfair treatment. I was even tempted to refuse to go. I had to pray for the strength to keep my mouth shut and trust in the Lord. I asked for the grace to let go of everything and die to my will and my plans. Through the grace of God, I kept making the act of faith that God would bring good out of it all.

The Lord showed me that my ministry was not what moved the hearts of people, but it was His grace and His power. The Lord showed me that Jesus had only three years of ministry, and he gave me 60 years of ministry. Jesus had only three years to preach and to evangelize, and His call was to evangelize the whole world.

Jesus could have objected to His call to suffering and death when He had just begun. He had to trust that the power was in His death and resurrection and not in His ministry and that others would carry it on. His disciples were not yet well formed and ready for Him to leave them. In fact, they were even going back fishing. This was no time to go to crucifixion and death. It might cause them to give up everything He had planned for them. Jesus even prayed, "Father take this chalice away from me." Then He made this decision to trust in His Father, "Not my will, but thy will be done." (Luke 22:42)

He decided to surrender and trust His Father. His suffering, death, and obedience to his Father had more power to convert the world than all of His miracles and preaching. I decided that it would be the same for me and that my suffering and death would have more power to save the people that I love than all of my preaching.

How did it all turn out? You know how it turned out for Jesus. Crucifixion and death and the cross are the real power of the gospel that has saved and changed the world. It was the crowning glory and power of His whole life and ministry. It opened the door to His Resurrection and Ascension into glory. For me, this move to Toronto, even though very painful and challenging, and a real death to myself has transformed me. I have grown more in holiness than I could even imagine I could do. I trust as I pray for everyone that the power of God goes out to him or her. God can use my trials and struggles and my prayer more than He could my ministry.

My ministry was often too much mine. It was self-fulfilling and a little bit proud and something that I would do for enjoyment, not just to help people. Things work for a greater good when I die to my will. The power is in our death, just like it is in Jesus's death and not only in what we do in our ministry. So this surrender and end to my plans and my power and myself and my wishes the last few weeks of my life here in Toronto have been the most significant thing that's ever happened to me. Jesus was able to use me and my little death and crucifixion, and he's blessed me with peace and strength and joy, not without considerable struggle and suffering. I praise him and thank him and rejoice in his goodness.

Since I now have serious health problems and constant pain in my heart, and I realize that my life is coming to an end, I thought I would say goodbye to everyone just in case the Lord calls me suddenly.

Wow, this is great! This time as I approach leaving, this world is unique and exciting. I am going back to God and we will, I pray all do this one day, for we all must leave this world. Jesus will continue to use me to bless and help all of you, even when I am heaven.

If we unite with Jesus, we will defeat death and rise from the dead with Jesus, because we are in love-union and faith-union with Him. But He may keep me alive for a few years yet. Only God knows. Someday I will go to the one from whom all of us have come, our real home, our Father, creator, and family.

I have a sincere regret that I was not a greater blessing to everyone and that at times I gave a bad example, and neglected to pray for others and to help them as I was called to. I was often very self-centered and too concerned about myself and my health, and my desires, and my happiness, and neglected to help others, as I should, and to pray for them as much as I should. I want to apologize and ask for forgiveness for my failure to be a faithful Christian follower of Jesus and a priest in the likeness of Jesus.

Jesus completely forgot Himself and lived for others and gave Himself entirely to others even to death on the cross to save them. I wish I would have followed Him and imitated Him, and given my life more for others as He did. In these last days or months of my life, I want to makeup and pray for everybody more and pray for you. I offer all the love of Jesus and His suffering and redemption for the salvation of all of you whom I've known and loved and, at times, failed to love completely.

Through His mercy and love and my faith in Him, I can bless everyone I pray for powerfully because all power is in Jesus, who is our God. So I pray for you and ask for your forgiveness and trust that the Lord will make up for all of my failures to love you and care for you. I pray that you, too, will see your need for God and trust in Him to bless the people that you care for and pray for. The real power to help and save others, and love, comes from our trusting prayer to God.

These last few months of my life, I will be in Toronto and will not minister as a priest except through my prayer for you all and offering mass for you. I trust in Jesus to use this to heal and bless you all. I pray that these words and reflections in this little book may be of help to you when you read them, and even if Jesus does not use them that He will bless you through others and in other ways.

I encourage you to keep working on your union with Jesus, for it must be a deep friendship and relationship closer than a marriage. We must keep working on our prayer life and spend quality time with Jesus just as we must do with our spouse or our best friend. If we die in love-union with Jesus, we will rise from the dead with Him and ascend into heaven with Him and share His glorious life forever.

When I think of the great love and mercy of God, I sometimes feel I'm going to burst with joy. I laugh, and I cry, and I pray, and I sing. All I can say is thank you Lord, thank you Lord, thank you Lord, thank you for your great love for me, and your mercy.

I give you my love and prayers in Jesus, which is the best thing that anyone can give!

Father Clair

Rejoice Always
52 Lessons on Joy

Joy is looking at the world through the lens of eternity. Understanding that there is beauty and purpose in or ordinary lives. That God uses those ordinary lives to accomplish great things in his name.

To use this book, find a comfortable spot. Maybe a corner of the couch, maybe your pillow at night, maybe at the kitchen table in the morning sun with a cup of coffee. Give yourself the gift of five minutes to read one of these reflections. To become part of our hearts and to create more joy in our lives, these little stories need to percolate. Reflected on them and revisited them. You can read the book straight through and then read it again, or repeat each reflection for a week. Wishing you more joy and peace as you come to know how much the God who created you loves you. Stay true to who you are, and then one day you will see with humble amazement that God used your willing, obedient, ordinary life. Say the little prayer below as you read each reflection.

Lord, please keep reminding me that You love me. I willingly offer You all that I am and all that I have to achieve your purpose. I choose to believe that who I am is important to You. I know where you are there is joy.
Jesus I Trust In You!

1. GOD IS WITH US IN EVERYTHING
As we trust in Him and pray.

Life is not just a series of uncontrolled happenings that we live. Life can have meaning and purpose. God knows what's going on. God is weaving the tapestry of your life, with us having a part to play changing it, and at times messing it up. The good news is, even if we mess it up, He can make it turn out beautiful in the end.

Our life has happy and sad times. However, nothing can come into our lives that He cannot change for the good, as we turn to Jesus and trust in Him to heal and forgive us. You are a child of God. He loves you. He is our loving Father, and He can bring good out of everything that happens as we trust in Him and turn to Him.

Don't misunderstand me. I'm not saying that everything that happens to us in life is God's perfect will. That's just not true. There are a lot of things that are not God's perfect will. If you sin, that's not God's will. If somebody sins against you, that's not God's perfect will.

But God does have a permissive will. If I go out and do stupid things, I pay the consequences. If I go out and wreck my body, I pay the consequences. God does not cause evil, and God does not cause suffering. But He does allow those things because they have a purpose. God permits them, and then He uses them, and can even bring a greater good out of them.

God, the Father, let his own Son suffer and die. Did God bring any good out of that? He brought the greatest good out of the worst thing that ever happened on the face of the earth. What could be worse than that people would torture and kill the very one that loved them into life?

God loves to turn crucifixions into resurrections. So how can you and I respond to painful or difficult things in our life? We can choose, by the grace of God, not to give up but to trust in the Lord. What would you say to someone who asks why God allows terrible things to happen to good people? Will God help you to trust and pray in the time of your trial and your suffering and pain? I know from my own experience that it is not easy, but through the grace and mercy of the Lord, I keep turning to Jesus. Even when I doubt and start to give up, He helps me get up again.

Over the last five years, I fell and broke my collarbone and five ribs and still cannot sleep on my side. Then someone threw a big rock and hit me on the head, and I was rescued from the mountainside and taken to the emergency by ambulance. Then a rolling car pinned my arm against another car and broke some bones and damaged some nerves. So lots of adventures, and somehow God was with me. Through it all, it helped me to grow in trust and patience, and faith, and to believe that He brings good out of everything.

Now I am having problems with narcolepsy and fall asleep all of the time in the middle of everything. So I pray, standing up and walking to keep awake. I also struggle with feeling tired and sleepy much of the time. Getting old and going through life isn't for sissies. We need God's help to have courage and peace in the midst of everything that comes. Jesus' life was not easy, nor was the lives of the saints and martyrs, or the prophets in the Old Testament.

We do not even admire someone who always has a soft life. But we do respect people who have the courage to remain at peace and in joy through trials and suffering. Is this not true?

I thank God for each event that comes into my life. When I catch myself grumbling, I ask the Lord to help me and renounce my' pity party'. My sufferings are so small compared with many people. He knows I am extra weak, but if my time comes for significant trials, He will be there for me when it happens.

The greatest gift is that I can see that God was there in each event, and used each occasion to draw me closer to Him. So now I thank God for each thing that has come into my life, and maybe the next thing is death, and I trust that He will be there to take me through it to Himself.

2. THE CLOCK

A view of eternity…

When I was young and living with my parents, there was no talk about God or prayer. Fortunately, there was a good priest in High River, Alberta, the town closest to our farm, and he had us baptized, but we did not go to church when I was very young. When I was six years old, my parents lost their farm because they couldn't make the payments, and we moved into town to live with my grandmother because my father was out of work during those Depression years.

Father Boland was the priest in High River, and he used to visit us even though we didn't always go to church. He got me to be an altar boy, and I went to serve at Mass, although I didn't like it. But I came to believe all the things that I heard, and it all made sense to me that there must be a God and heaven and hell and that we must die.

I didn't make it to catechism class that regularly, and I never did my homework or memorized the answers as the teacher told me to do, as the other children did. But when we had our little test and exam, I knew the answers by just thinking them out from what I understood better than all the others, even though I hadn't memorized them. Somehow I understood them even at that age of seven. The teachers were reluctant to give me the prize for getting the best marks because I did not provide the memorized answers, but I got the idea across on more of the questions. They finally decided to give me the prize but warned me that I would not get it again for the next test if I did not attend more of the classes.

I always had a philosophical bent. So I used to ponder life. The first realization of this was once when I was about eight years old. In my catechism, there was a clock, a big clock. It was supposed to be a representative of Time and Eternity. On-the-clock one minute block was marked and labeled our lifetime, and 24 hours represent eternity, and it said, compared with eternity, 100 years of life is about a minute or even less. So, for one minute, we will have human life, and for all the eternity, we will be in joy and heaven with God or separate from God and in hell. I have a very logical mind, and this touched me deeply, and I decided that I wanted to get to heaven. That was the most crucial thing in life. Why live for just one minute of life and lose out on an eternity of life. Then the question was asked what the critical thing about this life is? Would you want to spend all your energy and time on the one minute, or would you want to plan for the whole 24 hours? I realized that I wanted to live for eternity, not for just a minute of life in this world.

I realized the Lord is speaking to me and calling me. What is the essential thing in my whole life? It is to grow in love and holiness; to deepen my union with Jesus, my Lord. Everything else is only temporary and passing and gone forever.

I challenge you to make a retreat and spend some time with the Lord and seek His will. Your union with Him is everything, and it comes by communication and making time to be with Him. I believe people do this when they are very much in love, and they are with the one they love. They seem to be able to put aside everything, and their attention is entirely with the person they love. All that matters and all that exists is just being there in that moment with the one they love. In this situation, time seems to stand still. A whole hour goes by, and it just seems like a moment.

It would be hurtful if the one we love says to us, "Let's get our lovemaking finished. I've got other things to do." Do we say to God I want to get my prayer time with you finish because I've got other things to do?

Let us pray that you and I make a good deal of time for Him and hear his voice and be not afraid to follow!

3. SHOOTING STAR
God loves me. He really loves me.

I was born during the Depression in 1932. My father was bedridden, and we were desperately poor. My mother had one child, my sister, and then she was pregnant with me.

A social worker came out to our little shack on the farm that we rented. She said to my mother, "You have nothing, and no money to support your children, so why are you having another child? You can't even care for the one you have. Haven't you heard of birth control?"

My mother was deeply afraid, and so she decided to find out if she could get an abortion. In those days, there was no Medicare, so she could not go to a doctor. She looked in a magazine and found some advertisement for a drug that would cause an abortion. Someone gave her help to purchase this drug and so she did and took the drug to abort me.

She kept this a secret from everyone most of her life. But once, with a group in which everyone was sharing their personal experiences, she decided to get it off her chest and tell the people about her attempted abortion.

My mother was not able to nurse me, so I was not held very much but fed on the bottle in my crib. In my emotional life, I felt very worthless, rejected, unloved deep inside of me, and valueless. I did not realize that deep within me, I hungered to be loved, to be held, to be cared for, and to know that I did have value. I longed to be truly loved. I hungered for someone beautiful to love me. I believe everyone has this hunger to be loved by the Beautiful One, but my need, I think, was more profound and more unsatisfied than most.

24

Even in grades one, two, and three, I would get deeply attracted to one of the girls in the class and long to be loved by them. I would take a daisy flower and pluck the leaves one at a time, saying 'she loves me, she loves me not,' and if it turned out that 'she loves me,' I would feel a bit of joy; and yet I knew it was just a longing and a game but not real. However, the fantasy made me feel a little more love for a few moments.

When I was 4 or 5 years old on our farm, I went down to the barn to be with my dad, but he was busy and told me to get out of there. I felt deeply rejected, and I just wanted to run away. I just started walking away from my home, trying to get away from the pain, crying as I walked. As I went out into the field, through my tears, I spotted a flower. It was a flower our mother told us was called a Shooting Star. In some mysterious way, I sensed that flower was there as a sign that I was loved somehow by someone mysterious, and I picked it and held it close to me, as a sign that some incomprehensible reality loves me. It seems like a simple experience, but it was intense and profound, and it stayed with me all my life.

Many years later, when I was about 35 years old, I was feeling very unloved and lonely, having doubts about the existence of God. It was at night, and I was walking in the forest empty and with no sense of any purpose of God in my life. I looked up into the sky and saw all the stars, and I thought if there was a God, he might be up there in the sky someplace. So I looked up into the sky and said, "Oh God, if there is a God, and if you are there and you love me as Christians say you do, then give me a sign that you're there and that you love me. Give me a shooting star."

I thought, 'this is stupid, even if there was a God, who am I to ask for a shooting star? It would just be an insult to such a great being'. So I said, "I erase that prayer."

Something deep within me prompted me to repeat the prayer, still filled with doubt. I closed my eyes because I was afraid to look up into the sky, for I knew there would be no shooting star, and my depression would be more significant. However, I decided suddenly to look in spite of my fear and complete disbelief. To my amazement, there was a shooting star. Well, it just came over me, and I said to myself, "There is a God, and He loves me!"

But the joy only lasted a minute or two, and my logical mind took over and said, "Come off it, Clair. It is a clear night and what do you expect? It was just a coincidence that a shooting star should come at this moment. It doesn't mean that God is there or that He loves you. Don't be stupid".

Again something deep inside me asked and reasoned that it would be too coincidental if they were two come in a row. Then I would know there is no God because there wouldn't be another shooting star. So I shut my eyes and asked again for a shooting star, and then I looked with doubt and fear. To my amazement, another shooting star appeared. Again I had great joy, and I said to myself, "There is a God, there is a God, and He loves me!"

Then the whisper came again, "On clear nights there's often more than one shooting star. This doesn't prove a thing. It's just a coincidence."

So I was back where I started, and all my joy disappeared. Then the thought came to me, "Why not test it again then you will be sure there is no God and no one that loves you. If it happens three times in a row, it couldn't be just a coincidence."

So I repeated the request, with fear, and yet complete doubt. But I was amazed. Four shooting stars, shooting star after shooting star, appeared in the sky one after another. I broke down and wept and wept with joy.

I didn't get any sleep that night, and I prayed and rejoiced. I went to the church that morning, and as I was praying in the church, I started to laugh, and I couldn't hold it in because a voice was saying to me, "All your life, you didn't need to worry. I was there all the time, and you have no more worries, but now you know I'll bring good out of everything."

I had great peace and joy, and I was laughing at my problems and all my past concerns and disappointments. I think those in the church who heard me laughing, thought I was losing it, but I didn't care. All that mattered was that God loves me.

4. EMBRACE WHAT IS

In my life, when I look back at it, I see that the things that I thought were terrible and that seem to be very painful and destructive as I got closer to God and learn to trust in him, they all worked out to lead to my greater happiness.

I felt rejected by my parents. If I cried, my mother would say, "Stop crying, or I'll give you something to cry about." The first few times, I got taken in and said I wanted something to cry about. I thought I would get a cookie or something, but instead, I got a spanking.

So I decided that I better not cry anymore, and so I got into holding my breath to keep from crying. On one occasion, I held my breath so long that all my muscles must have locked, and so I passed out and turned all blue and started to turn cold. My parents could detect no signs of life, and so they were sure I was dead. They put me in the buggy and hitched up the horse and started driving into town to check with a doctor to see if I was indeed dead. Back with the bouncing of the wagon on the rough road to town, I started breathing again, and little by little, I began to revive and to come back to life and became conscious again.

These things gave me painful memories and wounds in my emotions. But as time went on, God turns them to the positive, for it gave me a humble heart, and I did not think of myself as great or important or valuable. Grace allowed me to turn to God in my emptiness, and he gave me love and new strength and the dependence upon Him. I have freedom from relying on human love and acceptance and the strength not to worry about rejection because I have him deep inside. It all works for good, and it has led me to greater happiness.

I was not accepted very well in school, and I was shy and fearful. That worked for good again as it helped me to graduate, look to God for security, and little by little He healed my shyness and gave me confidence.

Later on, I fell into the wrong crowd, and they misled and abused me sexually, and I got into great sin and guilt, in great pain, and worried that I would end up in hell, and I had lots of fear. But again, it led to my greater happiness because it helped me to keep praying and longing for mercy and longing to get out of sin because of my fear. God uses this to lead me to Him and happiness and peace once I went to confession and prayed and gained the strength to overcome my sin. If I hadn't had the fear and guilt, I would not have done anything about it, so the pain and the struggle worked for my good. I thank God for the pain and struggle, not because it was good in itself, but because God used it to lead me to Him and his happiness and peace.

For quite a while, I felt a little bit sorry for myself and brooded over my weaknesses in the things that happened to me, and I was angry with people that hurt me. But step-by-step, God helps me to let go of them and rejoice in the good. Now I can see that God was there with me. Little by little, He was leading me to get to know Him, to repent of my sins, to rejoice in his forgiveness and mercy.

I still get tempted when I get headaches or sickness to be a little distressed and want too much for things to change and to do something to get rid of my problem. I do not rejoice in what is, but struggle to change something that I think is worthless and only a problem and not helping me at all.

But then the Lord speaks to me, "You're not rejoicing. I'm in this. It will help you to be a blessing for others so thank me for what comes and trust in me that everything that I allowed to come into your life will lead to your greater happiness. You will unite your sufferings with mine for the salvation of the world and your salvation and happiness."

Then as I make an act of trust, I received some peace, and the headache and trials have purpose and meaning and do not bother me very much. I have a feeling of absolute peace and sometimes even joy in what comes and what God allows and gives me.

I keep trying to live the scripture "Rejoice always, pray constantly and give thanks in all situations for this is the will of God for you in Christ Jesus" (1 Thessalonians 5:16). I believe we all must try to do this. Even in the trying, when I failed to a degree, it is still a great blessing, and little by little, He helps me to live it more and more. I rejoice more and more and give thanks more and more, and I embrace every situation and everything that comes into my life more and more.

We might not always feel the trust or the joy or the thanksgiving, but we can decide to say it, and as we keep proclaiming it, even though it might seem untrue, if we make that decision, it is still very pleasing to God. And gradually, it will sink in, even to our emotions. We can say, "Lord, I want to trust in you and to rejoice and to give you thanks even though I don't feel it, I decided to trust that it is true that you will bring good out of it all even though my feelings are rebellious. Thank you Lord. I trust in you. This is my decision."

It may feel stupid and false, but by this decision, God is pleased. God is good and so merciful to me sometimes, it is overwhelming, and I laugh and cry and rejoice and sing because I've deserved nothing, and I have everything.

Pray that you could move in this direction. Take the scripture "Rejoice always, pray constantly and give thanks in all situations" as your model and your goal. Read it carefully, and write it out, put it up on your wall. You will be much blessed for doing this.

5. A PEARL OF GREAT PRICE

"The Kingdom of heaven is like a merchant in search of fine pearls; on finding one pearl of great value, he went and sold all that he had and bought it" (Matthew 13:45).

Jesus has become my pearl of great price, and I've come to realize that I am His precious pearl and that I am most valuable and beautiful in His sight. Jesus came to seek and win my love, which is His treasure.

You are God's unique, special pearl. You are beautiful in His sight, and very, very special to Him. He is seeking your love. He has a unique and great love for you that He has for no one else. Perhaps you are like me, because I often do not 'feel' precious, but I believe what the scriptures say. Jesus would not have come to earth and suffered and died on the cross for me if I were not very precious and valuable to Him.

Even if you were the only one on earth that needed saving, God would still have come to suffer and die to save you. I pray that we could come to believe in God's infinite love for each of us and trust in His love and great mercy for us.

Think of the love that parents have for their children. It is only a tiny image of His love, and He put that love in the hearts of parents. God is our Father, and He loves each of His children with an infinite and unique special love. He does not want to lose even one of His beloved children.

Say this often and proclaim it out loud, "I am God's beloved child. He loves me with infinite love and was willing to suffer and die on the cross to save me."

Have you figured out what scripture means when it says a pearl of great value, and to sell all that we have to get this treasure? This treasure is God's great love and mercy. We need to strive for it with our whole being. Likewise, you are God's treasure, and He gave up everything, even His life, to win the riches of your love.

In the end, only love can give us happiness and raise us from the dead, and fulfill all of our desires and longing, push out all fear in our life. We are created for love, and it alone can fill our hearts. "God is love" (1John 4:7)

Is love your goal for life, and are you growing in love? Do you love God and others more than a year ago? Make love your purpose for living and seek first the kingdom of God, which is love. Without love, there is nothing but emptiness.

Any love you have ever received, or seen, or given, is a little bit of God, for God is love, and wherever there is love, there is God, giving that love. He loves you with infinite love and would die on the cross a thousand times over to save you and win your love in return. Even if you betrayed Him over and over, and hurt Him again and again, He would still love you and forgive you and hope you would come back to Him.

Pray always, "Jesus; you love me more than all of the love that ever was on the face of the earth, help me to love you in return." This prayer has blessed me greatly.

6. THE GOOD THIEF

I want to share with you the greatest secret that I have discovered in the 86 years of my life.

A simple, profound truth, which has blessed me more than anything else: living life now. Because here is the mystery that we miss: all there is to life is each 'now' moment. There's a time of joy, and then it's gone. Then you have a time of sorrow, and then it's gone. There is nothing that exists and nothing you could ever do except what is done in the now moment. You can't do anything in the past – it is finished. You can't do anything in the future until it becomes the now moment. Everything is decided by your now moments of life.

Think of the Good Thief and the Bad Thief with Jesus on the cross, that 'now' moment. The Bad Thief looks at Jesus. He says, "Get me off this cross. This is pain. This is awful. If You are the Son of God, get me out of here."

He was locked in selfishness. He won't even look at Jesus, the innocent; he doesn't even see that He's not complaining. The Bad Thief also doesn't look at the Good Thief and asks that Jesus free him as well. But in that same' now' moment, the Good Thief opens his heart and says to the Bad Thief, "Look at this man, He did nothing wrong, and He is still suffering." Then he turns to Jesus and says, "Jesus, remember me when You come into Your kingdom."

In his now moment, the Good Thief chooses Jesus, to recognize His goodness, and to ask to be saved, not here in this world but for all eternity. The Bad Thief's eternity is also settled in that now moment.

The beautiful thing is that at any moment, you can turn to God, and you can be like the good thief. You can steal Heaven many times a day. Here's what I mean by that. I am going along in my life, and I kind of forget about God. I'm doing this and that I'm not thinking about God, and I'm moving a little bit away from Him. Then I realize what is happening, so I stop and say, "Lord, I want to choose You. In this now moment I want to give You glory. I want to trust You and be with You."

And just like that, I have salvation. I believe that at any now moment, if I am willing to repent, renounce the bad, and choose the good, then I have salvation. I think that every now moment has the key to Heaven. I believe we need to keep making that choice to follow God. God is so ridiculously loving and forgiving that even if I had been like the Bad Thief all my life if I truly repent and turn to Him, He would forgive me. Jesus is like the father of the prodigal son, foolishly loving, forgetting that the son squandered his money and ruined everything. That's why I find this an incredible secret because I can never get discouraged, and every day is a whole new life, a whole new chance to live for God.

Let's look at the Good Thief and Bad Thief and look at it as an example. Let's say we'd gone through life and wrecked everything, just like the Bad Thief, and we could be in utter despair: "I've wrecked my life and lost everything."

But God is so merciful that at that moment, life is so exciting because you can choose to turn to God. So I like to be the good thief at every moment of life, and I say, "Lord, at this moment of life, I want everything because I want You, and I want to renounce everything that is not of You, that is sinful, and I want to choose You now."

Then turn to Jesus and surrender in trust to Him, and then Jesus says to you, "This day you are with Me in heaven." You have Heaven within you for He comes within you to give you love-union with Him, which is Heaven.

I want to be the Good Thief and choose life. The temptation, though, to be the Bad Thief is strong: I might say 'I'm in pain. I'm so angry. I don't want this pain. I'm not going to turn to You. I just want to get out of this pain.' Or I could say 'no Lord; I'm going to trust You. You went through pain, the good thief and the bad thief went through great pain, I'm going to choose You Lord, I'm going to embrace it.'

It just makes life so exciting, because not only can I choose life, but every moment is a reward. God loves us so much that every moment of life leads to greater happiness if we keep choosing Him. Every time we choose Him, we grow in holiness, and we grow in the capacity to have joy. So I can say, "Wow, I have life today, I have eternal life this moment, I've got eternal life right now as I'm writing this. I want to do this for You, I want to do Your will, I want to trust that you will bless the people who will read this. I want to choose to love you and to always do Your will."

Every moment of life has a special grace because of God's love for me. Why do I believe this? I know in my heart, if I had a child and I had all power, I would plan that child's life so that every moment of his life led him to more capacity for the happiness I had planned for him because I want complete joy for the people I love. And if I, as a selfish person, want that, how much more does God want perfect joy for every one of us? He is love, and He created us for happiness, to be with Him.

7. HOW TO ALWAYS GET WHAT YOU DESIRE

Everything that God gives us is for our good and our happiness.

We as parents always want good for our children, and if we had the power, we would arrange everything to lead our children to happiness, and allow nothing that we could not use for our children's growth toward success and ultimate happiness. We might even allow our children to have some difficult times if they needed it to grow in strength and maturity, or also allow them to have a painful operation if they needed it for their health and to save them from final death.

Do we love our children more than God loves us, His children? Will we trust that He allows nothing to come into our lives without being there to bring good out of it?

"I consider that the suffering of this present time is not worth comparing with the glory about to be revealed to us." (Romans 8:18)

God so loves us that He gave His only son to be crucified for us. Will he refuse us the good things we need each day? He loves His only son Jesus and yet gave Him terrible suffering for a greater good and His glory in Heaven, and our salvation. All that comes into our life comes to lead us to glory and greater happiness. He sees us as another Jesus, but he is there for us to give us the strength and courage we need if we will trust Him and turn to Him.

Every day I get exactly what I want. How is that? It is because I have decided to want what God gives me each day, for I have decided that He loves me better than I love myself, and what He gives me is the best, for He has all wisdom and infinite love for me and He takes care of me. You can get exactly what you want if you decide to trust God and want what He chooses to give you each day and each hour.

What do you think? Will you embrace your life as it is, even the painful things, because you trust in His love and that He will bring good out of everything, even your sins and even out of the pain you caused yourself by your sins and disobedience? He loves you and will take care of you. Trust His love and see that in each thing in life, He is there with His treasure and strength for your profit and happiness. Decide to trust in Him and ask His help to embrace all that is in your life.

Most people want happiness, love, success, money, good food, various pleasures, a lovely place to live, friends, health, freedom from all pain and troubles. I think that nearly covers everything that most people seek and desire and want. How many people will achieve most of this? Not many will obtain much of these things, and even those who do achieve very successful and fulfilling lives, will get sick and die and lose it all. They, too, will end up with nothing.

The only people, with the fulfillment of their desires, are those who seek God and receive all of their desires in Heaven. I have only one thing that I want and ask from God. I tell God that I only need one prayer answered, and that is, "Grant that I may love You always and then do with me what you will." I need nothing else.

If I get this love for You Lord, I will get You and have You. You alone can give me perfect happiness! Things in this world will always be imperfect and even very painful at times, but God will wipe away every tear, and every sadness turned into joy. I decide that happiness comes from God and that I cannot raise myself from the dead and give myself eternal happiness. It is a gift from God given to me through faith and trust in Jesus as my saviour.

I have one other strong desire, I must confess. I want you to seek this gift from God with all of your heart so that you will receive eternal happiness and the fulfillment of all of your desires. I always pray for this gift for you and myself.

8. TRUTH BOOKLET

Here is an exercise that will give you a firm foundation and an anchor in the midst of the battles of life.

Keep a special anchor truth booklet, which you read and frequently proclaim so that in times of trial and attack, you will not waiver in your faith. Make a promise to God that you will never forsake this anchor of trust in Him and give in to the lies that may come your way and start to get a hold of you. Write out the truths about faith and God's love for you and that all things that come into your life or will come will be turned into stepping stones for your good and happiness as you cling to the truth of God's infinite love for you. It will keep you on the path to Heaven when various forces that come against you attack you.

Keep proclaiming the truth that the Lord loves you and wants you to be happy forever with Him in Heaven. Especially when you do not feel it is true. Feelings do no give us the truth. God is love and mercy. Whether we feel it or believe it does not change who He is. Our emotions lie and change with the wind of our experience, and Satan also lies to us and tries to get us to be angry and not trust in the Lord. Writing out these truths is something that I do and many others that I know. It leads to security and keeps you on the road to Heaven. I read it over as my creed of faith. I keep proclaiming it to myself, to God and to everyone who will listen. It is the anchor of my life.

Truths that we can have written in our "Truth Anchor Book":

• God will bring good even out of my sins and failures when I repent and confess them.
• With God's help, I will embrace whatever comes into my life and trust that God loves me and will be with me always.
• Even if I become sick and die, He will raise me up and take me to Heaven to be happy with Him forever.
• I can at any time be like the 'good thief' on the cross and turn to Jesus with faith in His mercy, and He will forgive me and place His love and mercy in my heart and restore my place in Heaven.
• Jesus promises that even "Though my sins are like scarlet, they shall be as white as snow" (Isaiah 1:18) and "as far as the east is from the west, so far has he removed our transgressions from us." (Psalms 103:12)
• Jesus promises that "I have loved you with an everlasting love" (Jeremiah 30:18)
• I always have the key to Heaven, which no power can take from me, and that is to repent and believe the good news of his love and mercy.

I write this because I do not want you ever to lose the truth of God's love for you!

9. THE LESSON OF AN ORANGE

There is such richness living in the 'now' moment.

I realized the power of the present one time in Lethbridge, Alberta. This morning I got up late, and I had to rush off to work at the University. I was very involved in putting on a big conference. It was a great deal of work, and I was way behind in all of the things that I had to do. Because I got up late, I was almost frantic with worry about everything. I thought that I would just grab an orange for breakfast and jump in my car and go. I had even neglected to say my morning prayers.

On the way out the door, I grabbed the orange to eat in my car while I was driving to work. But as I was going out the door, there seemed to be a voice inside me from the Lord saying, "Slow down. Stop rushing and go back into the house and sit down and eat the orange. You are so worried and upset about everything, and all you need to do is trust in me and sit down and eat the orange that I gave you."
I did not want to listen. My response was, "Aw, come on; this is crazy! I have enough problems without this nonsense! Forget it! I do not have time for this and how do I know it is you? I'm going!"

There was a battle going on inside of me. My resistance was strong, but something was pulling me to let go of my agenda and just try it. Through the grace of God, I said, "Okay, Okay. I will try it."

What a struggle. The rebellion deep inside of me meant I just did not want to let go of my plans and my agenda, but something moved inside me, and I went back into the house. I was on the verge of rushing out right away, but in some strange way, I felt I should try this.

So I sat down to eat my orange, and I started eating it rather quickly. The voice seemed to say, "Slow down. Eat slowly, a moment at a time. All I want you to do right now is to eat your orange. Don't always be rushing through things to get them done. Be present to the present moment. That is where I am."

I trusted that inspiration and prayed, "Lord, I'm going to trust this is you. You gave me the orange. I'm just going to enjoy it."

I took each piece one at a time, thinking how good each one tasted and how that was a gift of love from the Lord. I prayed, "Thank you, Lord, thank you for this orange. Thank you that I could slow down and eat this orange with you. Thank you that I could be with you, and thank you for all the different foods you created."

And isn't that strange, but that's one of the greatest memories of my life, just eating an orange. It tasted so good, and the Lord told me that life could be so beautiful and simple if I would just slow down and trust in Him; if I would just take one thing at a time and live the now, trusting in His love and presence. The Lord showed me that life could be so much more simple and joyful if I would let go and let God; if I would let Him be in charge and just take one thing at a time and trust in His love for me. All I need to do in lots of situations is to enjoy the present moment and do my present moment duty with faith and love, leaving the rest in His hands.

I will never forget the pure joy of letting go and just being with the Lord and enjoying my orange. Also of thanking Him that in love, He created that orange for me. I realized God created all good things because of His love for all of us.

Everything has precious value. Everything has a great reward if we could only live that way more, what a blessing that would be. Because life is a string of events, of duties, prayers to say, work to do. If we could do them more for God and enter into the moment and see the precious value, we would be so much better off. All of life contains these beautiful moments, precious jewels if we could live the 'now' moment and embrace them.

I was tempted not to listen, but through the grace of God, I decided to try it. It took a lot of effort. But I took a deep breath and let go and just took one piece of orange at a time and tried to be present. The orange tasted so good, and I realized it's better to live the present moment and rejoice in what God gives you. I felt a great peace that all I had to do in life is eat my orange--so to speak. And then do the next thing with an absolute peace knowing that God is there.

Sometimes I would lose all of this in no small degree, but then I would start again, and always it gave me a fresh new outlook on life whenever I'd be willing to let go and live in the now. Even as I type out this message, I'm trying to just be present to God here with me. I try to let the Lord be with me and pray for anyone who might read this that they could discover what I have found. Life is not something to get through, but it's something to live and experience in the present moment.

I share this with you with a prayer in my heart that you would try this and work on it. Just try to do it for one day or one hour and be present with God, who is in that 'now' moment.

10. MY LOVE STORY
Love isn't a feeling. It is a decision.

Perhaps our priest or our parents, or at least the saints and spiritual writers, encouraged us to love Jesus totally above all others. They encourage us to seek him ahead of everybody and everything else and to spend time talking to him in prayer daily and frequently.

It is what happened to me. I listened to the priest and read the saints, and I made time as a young person to pray. I grew very much in my relationship with Jesus. Jesus was seeking a love relationship and the total gift of myself in a covenant commitment. I resisted going this far. I had other things that I put first and captured my attention and desires. It took a long time, but Jesus finally captured my heart. He became the most important person to me, and I entered the seminary.

It was very much like a marriage. I was thrilled with my relationship with the Lord. Jesus became my greatest joy, and I loved being with him in prayer. I made a covenant commitment by my religious vows, which is the image of a marriage. I even wore a ring after I took my vows as a religious. I promised to remain faithful and to share life with Jesus for the rest of my life.

The honeymoon stage lasted two or three years. However, then things got rather dry, and I got interested in my work and other things and neglected my relationship with Jesus. It wasn't as attractive as it was for the first few years of my relationship. I was even tempted to leave my covenant commitment to Jesus and at times I was very attracted to a lady that I got to know and who was very attracted to me. Once I neglected prayer

Now I have to tell you the rest of the story and how I fell in love again and how the Lord pursued me and forgave my unfaithfulness. Jesus pursued me even though I neglected him, and I wasn't faithful to him and didn't make very much time for him. I often just went through the routine of talking to him a little and saying hello in the morning and saying a few routine words to him at night before I went to bed.

It was very much like some husbands and wives do towards their spouse when they lose some of the interest in each other. Couples often hold on to resentment if they have been hurt or go through the routine and stay together but have little joy in being together. They can become almost like strangers to each other. Others in their old age stay together and care for each other, but they do not have much enthusiasm or joy in their relationship.

At about that time, I had a good friend in Lethbridge whose husband had a stroke and ended up in the hospital entirely dependent. His wife (whom I will call Mary) went to the hospital every day and helped care for him. She helped the nurses by feeding him and washing him.

It went on for months and then years. Mary was always there for him every single day. I felt sorry for her, and I told her that she did not need to visit him that much. I said that he does not even recognize you, so it would not matter if you only came once a week or once every few weeks.

She rebuked me and said, "Father! What are you saying! He is my husband and I love him. He was there for me for thirty years. I am going to be there for him every day!"

It touched me deeply, and I realized what commitment and strength there was in real love. I realized that Jesus was there for me all of my life, even when I was cold and distant toward Him. I hurt Him deeply by my sins. Still, He never stopped loving me and caring for me. He would never quit seeking me. He suffered and died for me when I was sinning against Him. Who else would love me that much?

He loves you and seeks you the same way and has an individual unique great love for you that he has for no one else. Will you give yourself to him as he gives himself to you so the two of you could be one in glory in Heaven forever?

11. WHAT DO YOU DO WHEN SOMEONE HURTS YOU

What do you do when someone hurts you, and it is unfair to you?

Do you tell them a thing or two about it? Do you bawl them out? Do you tell others about how rotten they were to you? Do you go to other people for comfort and sympathy and tell them about the one who hurt you? Do you try to get back at them by saying angry things to them or others? Do you say to yourself, 'I will drop them from being my friend'? What do you do? Be honest.

What does Jesus want us to do? He says, "Love your enemies, bless them that curse you, do good to those who hate you, and pray for those who despitefully use you, and persecute you." (Matthew 5:44)
Jesus says," Do not resist an evildoer. If anyone strikes you on the right cheek, turn the other side. If anyone wants to sue you and take your coat, give them your cloak as well." (Matthew 5:38-39)

He says, What good is it if you just love your friends, even sinners do this, even those who are evil, there is no reward for that, but a great reward for loving your enemies because then you are like Jesus, a true Christian. "Everyone loves those who are good to them, so what reward is there for that? I say to you, love your enemies and do good to those who persecute you. Pray for those who speak against you and hurt you." (Matthew 5:44)

If we get all upset and angry when we are hurt and tell everyone about it we cause war as some will be on our side and be angry and fight for us and others will be on the other person's side and say it was our fault and it could divide the whole community. A verbal war breaks out or an email war. People become more and more hurt and angry and even bitter.

If we forgive even before a quarrel begins and work it out with our brother between the two alone and humble ourselves, then the whole community may remain at peace and not be destroyed. We are all sinners and all need to repent and forgive. Those who do the hurt must humble themselves and go to their brother and ask forgiveness, even if they feel they are only two percent at fault. Be humble, and the other side will be humble. We must be quick to humble ourselves and forgive as Jesus forgives us.

Every hurt is an opportunity to be forgiven by God and receive a great reward for letting go of the pain and giving complete forgiveness. Wow! I can get great mercy and forgiveness from God because I am going to be extra kind and forgiving to that person who hurt me.

Think of those who irritate you, or you avoid and dislike, and the rejected who are unloved by nearly everyone. Love for those who seem the most unlovable is the heart of being a follower of Christ. You believe that everyone is a child of God. We are all His precious children loved by Him. Jesus said, "Whatever you do to one of these, the least of my brothers, you also do unto me." (Matthew 25:40)

Jesus died even for those who crucified Him. He loves even the worst sinner. Jesus loves you and me with infinite love. We are to love as He did. This is my commandment, "Love one another as I have loved you." (John 13:34)

We cannot do this by ourselves. We need Jesus' love inside of us. He will love in and with us as we decide to surrender to Him, and want this kind of love and keep asking for it.

Do you want to love others as Jesus does? God will give you this gift if you're going to keep asking and seeking it. Pray for the heart of Jesus, for those who hurt us, for the unloved, and those who seem unlovable. (Some times I am miserable and unlovable!)

Let us pray that we can do this. The Lord will help us!

12. CONFESSIONS OF A PRIEST

God's grace brought me to Him.

I didn't like going to church or being an altar boy, but I had this deep intellectual faith. Then I made an almost fatal decision; I would wait until I was old, and then come to God and prayer, and I wouldn't bother with Him until then, because it wasn't any fun and I didn't enjoy it. So I quit going to church and being an altar boy, unless my parents took me to a church, as they sometimes did. This decision almost destroyed me because I got in with a wrong crowd that taught me all kinds of things that were evil and destructive, and I forgot all about God.

Then we moved to Calgary, and my parents sent me to a Catholic School, not because they had that much faith, but because they heard that the Catholic school was the best and their whole ambition was for me to get a good education so I wouldn't be poor like them the rest of my life. But I had a powerful conversion in the Catholic School when we made a retreat, and a Redemptorist priest gave a powerful 'Hell and brimstone' sermon, about how mortal sin will destroy you.

I was terrified and feared hell, and so I wanted to go to confession, but I was too afraid to make an honest confession. I worried about this so much that my body even broke out into a rash, and finally, I dared to make a good confession. Then I had great peace and joy.

I decided I wanted to become a priest to make sure that I didn't get back into sin again. The Basilian priests that taught me were friendly to me and used to invite me over to their house where I played pool and Ping-Pong with them, and one of the young priests used to play football with us. I thought this is a pretty soft, easy life, and I would have it pretty good in this world and stay out of trouble and get to heaven too. But I had no desire to preach or evangelize or help others to get to heaven.

By the time I got to grade 11 and 12, my life was going quite good. I went to Mass regularly even when my parents didn't go, and I committed to saying the rosary every day. I thought that I could get to heaven without being a priest; I wanted to fly airplanes and shoot up targets like the movies I watched of the Second World War. I applied for Royal Roads Military School to get into the Air Force, the RCAF. I won a scholarship and had my ticket to go to military school.

Near the end of August, when I already had my ticket to Victoria for military school, I had to walk by one of the Basilian priests, and I told him about my plans. He said to me, "I thought you were going to be a priest?"
I didn't want to displease him, so I said to him, "Well, maybe I'll do that later after I'm through with the military."

He said to me, "Well, if you're going to be a priest, you should do it now because you won't ever decide to do it later," and then he walked away.
I remember this very vividly, and I was standing in front of the cathedral in Calgary, St. Mary's Parish, where I attended. All of a sudden, I thought, "What will I wish I'd done when I'm 80 years old and getting close to death?"

In about two or three minutes of standing before the church, I made a decision not to go to military school and went to apply to go to the seminary to become a priest. My parents were distraught and said it was crazy to change my mind at this stage.

The Basilian priest said I was too late to enter the novitiate that year. I did not give up, and by the grace of God, I was finally admitted. In the interim, I had a profound encounter with the Lord that all I wanted to do was pray. It gave me great joy, which I had never experienced before. God's grace brought me to Him.

13. THE WAY TO HAPPINESS

Love bears all things, believes all things, hopes all things, and endures all things. 1Corinthians 13:7

How about you? Do you bear all things and even embrace what God gives you as Jesus did, or do you complain? Get me down from this cross. I hate this, and I cannot stand that. Or Jesus, you accepted what God allowed. Who am I to complain?

We are all suffering, you, Jesus, the Good Thief, and the Bad Thief, and me too. Which of the three will I be? Will I be the one who complains? Or will I be the one who embraces my trials and sufferings for the salvation of those I care about and for the world? At least I could turn to Jesus and ask for help as the Good Thief, and I may have heaven soon.

This love which embraces the situation that comes now, whose source is God's very self, is an open heart, and a trust in His merciful love. When you're in that trusting space, you have some peace, grace, and redemption flow out of you to others. When you're not trusting in God and His love and mercy, then you lose peace and are discontent and even angry.

It's all about who did me wrong and why I don't like 'those people.' Any time you feel like you deserve better, 'poor me,' it is so unfair; it may mean you may be a selfish taker and not a giver or a lover. The temptation is to close down, to judge and dismiss and hate and fear if you don't have trust in the presence of God's love and mercy to bring greater good out of your life experience, even while suffering and almost a crucifixion.

You have to strive to live in love, to have a generosity of spirit, a readiness to smile, a willingness to serve, which comes through prayer and constant decisions to renounce the negative and choose to trust in God's great love for you. He will forgive you always and help you if you keep praying and asking Him to come. Faith and trust open the door to love, peace, and security. Regularly check in with yourself, asking, "Is my heart open? Is love flowing from me? Am I praying and trusting and turning to God to help me?"

Our culture seems to be sucked into a world of selfishness, just the opposite of real giving love. Always taking and wanting more for self. We have more material things than any ever had in the history of the world, and yet, because of our greed for self, we are less happy. By daily practicing real prayer from your heart and genuine desire to love, then sooner or later, you fall into love; and then you live your life in Jesus. You live no longer for yourself but for God and others. Keep seeking the joy of true love, and you will find it. It is the gift of God.

Love is a choice. You have to choose to love. You have to deliberately keep choosing to stay in contact with Jesus through your prayer. Jesus is the source of love, which is the heart and very life of God. It is something I see in others and have experienced, and I know it is real. I send this call to you for your happiness.

14. A CURE FOR SADNESS

I have discovered an antidote for depression and sadness and worry.

I thank you, Lord, for revealing this to me and helping me with it. I feel that what causes me to be worried, and a bit depressed is thinking negative. When my health is not right, or I'm not able to pray very well, and many things are going rather badly, I get worried and feeling down. I start thinking, "I can't take this anymore, and everything is falling apart."

It is my negative thinking that causes the unhappiness more than the actual pain or struggle. When I start proclaiming the truth, that God is with me and will bring good out of it all and that He will help me to handle this, and He will bring me through this, then I feel a lot better. Sometimes I have to keep saying over and over, "Lord, you love me, and you will take care of me. You are with me right now. You will bring me through all of this, and you will not abandon me."

God has given you a promise that you will have everything you need to make you happy forever in heaven. You have the word of God, and the promises of Jesus, that He will bring you through all the trials and difficulties and struggles of this life. If you believe this, why shouldn't you have joy in your heart if you fully trusted in Jesus and the word of God?

I found out that if I keep proclaiming this truth about God's infinite love for me, and what He's promised me as it sinks in, I have more peace and joy because I have heaven already in my heart because Jesus is in my heart in His love and mercy. Jesus promises me that if I eat His Body and drink His Blood, I have life everlasting, and He will raise me up on the last day and take me to heaven where I will have perfect happiness forever. Why should I be sad if I believe all of this?

Sometimes I am overcome with joy and thanksgiving because I deserve nothing, and God in His mercy has given me everything. I found out that if I want to receive this joy and faith and trust, I must make time for prayer and meditative thought. I must think of the evidence that the saints give and the miracles witnessed, read about them, and keep praying.

At times even the saints in their emotions had strong feelings of doubt. But they had joy because deep inside, they knew the truth, and they would come to experience joy and peace again later after the time of trial.

Please try to proclaim the truth, and it will sink into your heart, and life will be more hope-filled and joyful!

15. I GET 365 LIFETIMES A YEAR

I try to live each day as if it were my first day, my last day, and my only day.

God gives us only one minute and one day at a time, and as we live the day so we live our whole life. Even if the day is like a crucifixion, we can be like the good thief on the cross with Jesus and steal heaven that day, and it can be the best day of our life, and we can receive Jesus that day and receive heaven that day.

At the end of every day, I repent of all my failures and give it all to Jesus and prepare for sleep as if it were death and entry into heaven because I repent and trust in Jesus to redeem everything and bring me to heaven if I die during the night. Then I rejoice and thank Him for everything because He brings good out of everything as I turn to His mercy.

Please try it and imagine you were born into life in the morning and had one day to prepare for heaven and to do good and pray and live the day for God and then die. The past is just a memory, and you have this one-day of life to live and prepare for heaven. Pretend God revealed to you the end of the world was coming tonight night, and He was giving you this one day to live for him and to bless those you love and that He judges your whole life on this one day and how you lived the day.

It is not just pretending because there is truth in it. All there is to life is the now. The past does not exist anymore, and the future has no existence until it becomes the now. Try this just for one day as if God gave you this revelation.

Think about it, as you live your day, so you live your whole life. Life is just this day, this day, this day, and it becomes your entire life.

---

16. DO YOU LOVE STANLEY

Whom do you love? Do you love Stanley Jones? Do you love Shirley Peters?

You probably do not love either one. Why is that? They are wonderful and loveable, and yet you do not love them.

Of course, you do not love them, because how could you love them if you do not know them very well or perhaps not even at all. How could you know Stanley and Shirley if you have not spent time with them, and allow them to reveal themselves to you? You might even learn to love them if you spent a lot of time being with them. Isn't that true? They must be revealed to you before you can love them. Perhaps you could at least admire them if you read a lot about them, and you may get interested in finding out more, and even meeting them.

Do you love Jesus above everything else? Do you love God, the Father? Do you love Mary, the mother of Jesus? You cannot love them very much unless you know them and spend time with them, and let them reveal themselves to you so that you can realize how beautiful they are and how much they love you. Go back and read what is needed to love Stanley and Shirley. The same rules apply.

God, and Jesus and Mary, know you very well and are with you all the time, and they love you greatly. Jesus loves you infinitely, enough to suffer and die on the cross for you, even though you have hurt Him, and also use His name as a swear word and disrespect Him. He still loves you.

If you want to get to know God and see His beauty and love Him, you could decide to seek Him and ask Him to reveal Himself to you and help you to desire Him and spend time with Him. He could capture your heart, as He has done with all of the holy people and saints. But perhaps you do not desire or want that enough to go for it?

I am full of the desire to save people from being captured by the world and not by Jesus. Scripture says that you cannot love both God and the world. Because I want you to be saved and to be happy is why I am sharing this with you and praying that you will see that you need to love God with your whole heart to have joy and peace.

17. STOP AND GREET THE ONE WHO LOVES YOU
The one who loves you is in you and gives you life!

Try stopping before each task and thing you have to do for the day, and try to say a brief prayer and offer the task at hand to the Lord and for the salvation of those you love. This simple practice can change your whole life and make it fruitful.

It only takes a few seconds, but it is not easy to remember to do it. Satan will do everything he can to stop you. I sometimes set a little alarm to ring each hour, so I will remember to stop and enter into God's presence for a moment and offer Him my life and my work.

Do not get discouraged. It is excellent, even if when you start, you only do it once or twice. It is still great and powerful to talk to God and to be for a moment in His awesome presence. It blesses the ones you pray for powerfully. It can grow and become very powerful and transforming, even if it starts very small, like a mustard seed.

(I stopped typing right now and prayed for you.)

18. WE ARE WEAK

Do your failures, weaknesses, and sins discourage you?

To understand God's great mercy and love, think of yourself as a father or mother. How do you react to one of your children who have many weaknesses and sins? I believe that a parent's heart goes out to the child most in need of help. God is the same way. Jesus came to call sinners. He came for those in most need of mercy.

It's important not to get down on yourself and discouraged by your weaknesses and failures. We need to trust in the great mercy of God. He even asks us to forgive one another 7 times 70. How much more will he forgive even though we fail many, many times? Yes, we have to keep trying and starting again. We must be willing to pray and do the best we can.

As we trust him and let him work in us and with us, and rely on His grace and mercy and love for us; only then can we get the victory. We will not get this victory on our own but through His grace and mercy. Even Saint Paul, who was incredibly strong and courageous, says that God's power has full scope in his weakness. (2Corinthians 12:5) Accept your weakness. God can bring good even out of your weakness and sinfulness. Trust in his mercy that is greater than all our shortcomings.

Here is what Saint Therese says: "I am not disturbed when I see myself as weaknesses itself. On the contrary, it is in my weakness that I glory."
She goes on to say that she expects each day to discover new imperfections in herself. Saint Paul says this same thing.

In my own life, I see not only weaknesses but sins and stupidity, and many, many failures. My temptation is to get down on myself and be disgusted with myself. Through Saint Therese, I am learning to laugh at myself and thank God for all my weaknesses because it makes me rely on Him and realize that without Him, I'm nothing but weakness and sin.

Do you despise yourself and brood and worry about your weaknesses? I do and have to fight against it. We don't come to God by eliminating our imperfection, but by rejoicing in it because it makes us aware of our need for God's mercy and love, and it keeps us humble.
St Therese called this her "Little Way," a way that everyone can follow. Therese's method is the way of being aware of your need for love and help from others. You must be willing to give yourself to God's loving embrace like a child abandons itself with confidence and love into the arms of its loving parent.

You may want greatness so you can be admired for what you have accomplished and not give God the glory. God has true greatness for you, but you may not be able to see it fully in this world, and it may not feel very grand.

God can turn our biggest failures and weaknesses and handicaps, and even our worst sins, into our greatest blessings. I see this in my own life because if I had been strong and successful and free of any shameful sin, I would have been proud, and I would have looked down on others and judged myself better and superior. I would have ended up self-satisfied and taking credit for my goodness myself, in pride.

I would not have found the truth that apart from God's special grace and help, I can do nothing but sin. I would have been lying in the face of God, thinking that I made myself great and successful. The truth is that the only thing I can do all by myself is sin and mess up the good God put in me.

Do I do everything for 'me' to be great, or do I forget 'me' and help others? Loving others and helping them is true greatness. It is the greatness of God. Maybe we do not even want this true greatness but only our selfish glory and self-admiration.

St. Therese once told her sister, Celine, who was upset with her faults, "If you are willing to bear serenely the trial of being displeasing to yourself, then you will be a pleasant place of shelter for Jesus."

If you look carefully at yourself, you will see how hard it is on you to not 'like' or respect the 'you' that God created. It is the initial emotional snag that sends you into bad moods without your knowing why.

St. Francis tells us to let go of the very need to "think well of yourself." That is your ego talking, not God. Only those who have let go of their false self-love can do this, of course.

Now it is essential to see the other side. The real you that comes from God and is in God is a beautiful, glorious child of God made in His image. We all have left our true 'self' and God and tried to be our own 'great creation,' and apart from God, we only create corruption and emptiness and sin. We can only produce good and beauty 'in' and 'with' God.

Jesus is our saviour and saves us in our weakness and sinfulness. That is what He is continually doing for me. To Him be all of the glory, and He will take care of me in His mercy when I deserve nothing.

---

19. THE BLESSINGS OF A FLAT TIRE

I wish to tell you another story from my own life that would illustrate the 'now moment.'

One time I was driving from Calgary down to Lethbridge for an important meeting, I believe it was a charismatic meeting, and I needed to be there. I was watching my time, trying to rush. I'm speeding a little bit trying to get there on time. As I am driving, a snowstorm starts. All of a sudden, I hear thump, thump, thump. I had a flat tire!

Well, I was so upset, as you can imagine. I'm going to be late. I turned to God, and I was kind of irritated, "Why would You allow this Lord? I have this important meeting, and it is about your work, Lord."

I'm like the Bad Thief on the cross, complaining about my lot. I get out, and it is very cold, probably -25C. Then I said, "Okay, Lord, I will just change this tire fast and speed a little bit more and maybe only be a little bit late."

I think that if I just hurry enough, it will all be okay, so I rush and open the trunk, getting the tire out, but I'm having trouble because it is so terribly cold. Finally, I have to stop and get back in the car to warm my hands. It was just an awful experience; I am getting more and more angry. Some bad words are coming to my mind. And then the Lord, in His great mercy and love, seems to speak to my heart.

He said, "I want you to let go, kneel down and just pray. Let go of your agenda."

And I said, "Oh no God, are You crazy? Is that You?"

It seemed like it was him. So I knelt, in the cold, on the pavement in the snow. And I said, "Lord, okay, I'm going to try to surrender. I surrender, but I don't want to surrender. I have to decide this now moment. Lord, help me. Help me. It's hard. I don't want to let go. I want to be there at the meeting. I want to trust you, Lord. I'm going to trust you, Lord, that You are with me, with this flat tire, in this moment of life. You can make it better than if I got to that meeting that I have been preparing for so long. I'm going to let go with your help, Lord. I let go. Help me let go. I just want to be here, embrace what is, this flat tire, this cold day, and this blowing snow. If I don't get there, it's okay."

Little by little, I started to have a peace and a joy. I thought, "I don't need to get my way. I can just accept in the present whatever God gives me, and trust that He will bring good out of it. That's what it says in Scripture in Romans 8:20 'All things will work for good as we love and trust God.' Lord, You will bring good out of this."

This moment, this little time that seemed like a disaster because all my plans were ruined is a highlight of my life. Isn't that crazy? It is one of the best things that ever happened to me. It helped me to learn the lesson of the 'now moment.' I will never forget it. I tell this story everywhere.

If you surrender to God, each moment of life can be a bit of a highlight. It was a real highlight because it took a lot of struggle, and it was the grace of God that I could let go. Then I just took my time, warmed my hands, and got the tire changed. I don't have to be at the meeting, I can praise you Lord and be with you, and you're in charge. You will bring good out of it. Wow. What grace. What a lesson in life.

—

I don't have to have my will; I can say your will be done. It's like you in the garden, praying, "Father, take this chalice from me. It is the worst thing ever. I'm going to be beaten and spit on and arrested." And then, You surrendered. "Not my will, but yours be done." Of course, mine is a lot easier, I don't get a lot of suffering. I got the tire changed. I didn't freeze to death. But it's still a beautiful moment, Lord.

I believe that every moment of life may not be a great highlight, but it still can be very beautiful. I just see the joy of each moment of life, even the simple little things. That is the real secret; not to just get through things, but to be there with God in each thing you do.

20. SPILLED MILK

It seems that sometimes when I am in a rush, and things don't seem to be going that well is when God comes in, and things go better than ever.

When I got older and read De Casados book "The Sacrament of the Present Moment," I started trying to live a day or an hour at a time as if that's all there was. I was not very successful for years. But sometimes when everything was going wrong, and I was in great pain and difficulty and worried about many, many things I would say 'pretend you only have one hour to live' and in this pretense, I would just focus on the 'now,' and all my troubles would start to melt. I kept pondering and thinking about this deeper reality that all there is, is now. The past is gone and doesn't exist, and the future is yet to come. Everything that happens in the now moment and at this moment we decide our eternity.

Every now moment of our life, if we decide to do the loving thing, God who is love comes more into our life. If we do the unloving thing, God will move more out of our lives. So I was in a rush again. I figured I better go without my meal, so I thought I better grab a glass of milk before I hop in my car. I reached in and grasped the pitcher, and it slipped out my hands and broke on the kitchen floor; glass and milk everywhere.

"Oh, man. It's going to take me a long time to clean this all up. But the housekeeper comes today, and she's a good sort, she won't mind cleaning it up. She gets paid to do it. I'll just leave it for her."

I started out the door. But my conscience said, "Wait a minute, you can't just walk out and leave that mess, even if the housekeeper doesn't mind, she's a good heart. But you've got to do what is loving and not leave that mess for her. She's got other things to do."

"Yeah, but I'm in a hurry."

"You've got to do what's loving. Or are you going to do the selfish thing?"

I went back in and was still a little grumbly; because I tend to be selfish and try to avoid things I don't like doing. "Okay, I'm going to try to do this Lord with my whole heart, please help me."

And it's the craziest thing because it became a highlight, a real highlight. I just took the glass up; I cleaned every drop of milk. I'm just going to do it for you, Lord, this little sacrifice, small as it is. I should have jumped to it right away and not even worried about it, but thank you that I conquered a little bit of selfishness because I tend not to do the thing I don't like doing.

God's grace came and blessed me. I always remember that. And this is as good as anything I'll ever do in my life because that's what life is, letting go of the selfish thing, letting go of your agenda, and doing the loving thing, doing your duty in the present moment. That's life, that's beautiful. That cleaning up the glass and the milk is as beautiful as any moment in my life will ever be. The more I do it with faith and love, the more beautiful it is. All of life contains these beautiful moments, precious jewels if we could live the now and embrace them.

21. PRAYING IN TRAFFIC

My life becomes more meaningful, even in the mundane tasks, by living in the 'now' moment.

Here is an example from my own life to help explain this concept of living the 'now' moment. I was a chaplain at a university and had to drive 15-20 minutes to work. I would try to make the green lights. Sometimes I would hit a bit of a traffic jam. I would get a bit irritated. "Oh, man, I wish I lived closer to work. Oh, look at that person, a slow driver." Try to pass them, hit a red light again. Try to make the green one. The drive was kind of a pain in the neck, and I would often be late and frustrated by the time it was over.

Then all of a sudden, I realized God gave me these 15-20 minutes; it's a part of my life. Why just throw it away? I wondered if I could do something worthwhile on this journey. So I started praying as I drove. If someone were in my way, I would pray for that person. I would think, "Oh good, a red light I could just be quiet for a moment and call down God's mercy. I can say a Hail Mary." Pretty soon, those 15-20 minutes of going to work became a highpoint of my day; the more I tried just to live that time for God. And somehow, as I worked on it, that became one of the most precious times in my life. I enjoyed it, and I was happy if it was a little longer than usual. Get tied up in traffic for half an hour, and I get to pray more and spend more time with God.

And then I got thinking, "Why can't I treat more of my life like this?" The more I start living and seeing the value of the 'now' moment God gives me, the more full my life becomes. Every moment is a precious gift from God. Every morning I get up and think that this is a whole new life: a beautiful day given to me by God. He just gives me one day at a time, one hour at a time, even one minute at a time. This gift of life for this day is beautiful. Give us this day our daily bread. I look at the Word of God at what Jesus said, "Don't worry about tomorrow, for tomorrow will worry about itself" (Matthew 6:34). Because that is what life is. It is now. That 'now' moment, really sets me free to do God's will in each 'now' moment.

22. DOING THE DISHES
Do you do very important things frequently?

I believe you can because every little thing done for God is very important and powerful and has a great reward. You can tell what is important to someone by asking them what they think about the most, and what they make time to do with most of the day. But above all, why are you doing this? If this world is the most important to someone, then they think about the most; the material things of this world and the concerns of this world and the things they want in this world. It is the natural thing to live for this visible world and to spend our time and thought on all the elements of this world and not spend much time thinking about our soul and the things of God and heaven.

The saints' concern, thoughts, ambitions, energy, and choices are focused on the things of heaven. They concentrate on the things of God. They do all of the little worldly things for God and that makes each thing important. Everything you do just for this world you will lose and end up with nothing; no material thing when you die. Everything done for the spiritual world, for God, heaven, and love of God and others, will last forever and has an almost infinite reward and will give you happiness forever. You will never lose any of it, as you will the material things, and concern about them.

It took me a long time to see this fully, and I often got caught up more with this world, and it was a complete waste of time and robbed me, and I could have lost everything and have nothing to show for it forever. But then I began to see and started to do more and more things; things for spiritual motives and love of God and others. It will last forever in heaven and have a reward beyond our imagination.

Do not misunderstand me, we can and must do the material things for material needs, but the primary value and motive must be for God and His blessings. A simple example is, we still do the dishes to get them done, but we can do this and offer it to God and see that its central importance is not just, so we have plates for the next meal, but for love of God and in obedience to what He wants. Even just giving someone a glass of water, if done in God, will not go without its reward, but if done with no reference to God, and completely separate from any desire to serve and please God, then it has no value or reward.

Even one prayer said, perhaps while doing some task needed will have a very, very great reward, and we will never lose it if we learn to seek first the things of God. It is a beautiful secret that I have learned, and it gives meaning and importance to everything I do in this world. Even the small little unimportant things I do, take on high value and relevance, as I offer them to God in a bit of prayer.

I never do this very perfectly, but it is such a joy even to offer my failures to God and trust that He in His great mercy and love is pleased and rewards me!

23. GLORY BE TO THE FATHER
I learned this lesson of life

Life can be more and more meaningful if I can just do the duty of the moment in love and faith and, if possible, with a little bit of prayer, even when it's dry.

When I say the Glory Be's sometimes, it can seem a little dry, and it doesn't seem like anything that great. I say, "Oh Lord, it means even more if it doesn't feel exciting. Oh Lord, it is even more beautiful if it doesn't feel good, if it feels dry, if I say it just out of love, in the dryness. Oh Lord, this is good, this is beautiful. I'm going to say a Glory Be, and I don't feel it like I sometimes do. I don't feel I'm giving you glory. It just seems like a dry saying of the words: Glory be to the Father and the Son and the Holy Spirit. I want to give you glory in the dryness. You deserve the glory even when I don't feel it. I know it's beautiful because anybody would give you glory if they feel excited about it. Anybody can say an excited Glory Be. But I get to say a Glory Be when I feel no excitement. No desire to say it, just a dry Glory Be. But I want to do it in love because love isn't a feeling it's a decision. Glory Be to the Father and the Son and the Holy Spirit. As it was in the beginning, it is right now, this moment, glory to you forever. Thank you, Lord."

We can't always, at least I can't, live life fully, as I do on some occasions. Sometimes it's dry, and it seems humdrum. But I keep making that act of faith. Lord, this is just as exciting as when I felt it with the tire, the spilled milk, and the orange. I'm still going to give you glory in the dryness when it's just an ordinary thing. I'm still going to make that act of faith that this is a precious moment. Each moment of my life has a value, and I'm going to offer and live each moment as best I can, to the full.

—
74

It is the secret that I want to share with you. Try it. Even if I only do it once or twice a day, it's still beautiful. Then if I can do it three times a day, four times, even five, life starts to have more meaning. Each day has more meaning. As I try to live it with God and embrace each moment, He gives me, even the painful ones, even the boring ones.

24. WHY ARE MY PRAYERS NOT ANSWERED?

The Lord said. "Whatever you ask in my name, the Father will give it to you." (John 16:23)

Many people find this very difficult to believe because they asked for many things, and they do not receive it. How do you explain this? Here is the way that I understand it. Let us look at a human image. If I asked my human father for $500 and he does not give it to me until three months later, he still heard my prayer and answered it, even though I may have doubted that he was going to help me.

It is the way I think it is with God. Let us say that we ask God for healing from a disease that we have. And then nothing happens. Then later, He gives us the healing. Well then, his words are correct, we asked, and we did receive, even though we had to wait.

I believe that everything good we ask for, and all the healing and all the riches we might ask for we will receive in heaven, but we have to wait. Many times it is His will to provide us with many gifts here on earth, but this is a sign to help us and not the main answering of our prayers.

On earth, He gives us some of the things we ask for, at least some of the time, but then we will lose it all and die. However, if we have to wait to receive it in heaven, we will never lose it and never die and never get sick again. Consequently, it is better to get our healing and riches in heaven because if we get this on earth, we will lose it all. In heaven, we will keep all of His gifts forever; so which is better?

It is a real test of our faith when we have to wait, but He will help us. Will you choose to trust Him when you have to wait? I decide to trust God and know that everything I ask for, that is really for my happiness and my good, God will give this to me in heaven, and I will never lose it. He wants my joy even more than I do.

I was always kind of the intellectual doubter about God doing miracles. I knew of a lot of answered prayers that seemed like a miracle, but it wasn't conclusive. Here is a story of how an answered prayer was a miracle for me.

Shortly after I was ordained, I was in Kelowna, British Columbia, where my parents lived. It was Saturday, and I was to say one of my first Masses that Sunday. I went out on a boat with my brother that Saturday afternoon. While out on the lake, we decided to jump in and go for a swim. I had knocked out one of my front teeth and had a temporary plate with a tooth on it. When I jumped into the lake, I coughed out my tooth into the lake.

We rode back to shore, and everyone was laughing because, with my missing tooth, I had a lisp. I said to myself I couldn't say Mass like this; everyone will laugh. My brother and I got back into the boat and rode out onto the lake, hoping and praying that we could find the place when I jumped into the water, and so find my tooth. Everybody said it was impossible and foolish even to try. But I was kind of desperate. I thought perhaps I might receive help from God since I had to say Mass. I said a little prayer, asking for help.

I dived into the water and tried to go down to the bottom, but it was too deep. However, I thought I saw something white on the bottom of the lake. By this time, the waves had moved the boat, so I thought, how am I going to find the same place again. Then the thought came to me if God is doing this; it doesn't matter where I dive-in. This time I made it to the bottom, deep as it was, and I took a handful of sand where I thought I saw something white and came up. When I opened my hand there in the sand was my tooth. When I got back to the house, everyone was amazed, and I was happy that I could speak without everyone laughing.

I pray that the Lord will give you and I faith and trust in Him, that he does hear our prayer, and that one day we will see this. More things are answered by prayer than this world could ever dream of or realize. In heaven, we will see this! Let us pray for each other that we would never lose faith and trust in God no matter what happens.

25. SHOW GOD A LITTLE LOVE

In each moment, we can show God we love Him. It is the little things we do.

I'm kind of a coward, and sometimes I am a little bit lazy and stubborn. Sometimes I go to say my night prayers, and I rush through them because I am tired. I say the Hail Mary, and then I jump into bed, thinking how tired I am. Then the Lord says to me, "Hey, you kind of rushed through those prayers. You didn't really pray them very much. Why don't you get out of bed and pray them again?"

"Oh, Lord, I'm tired. I can pray them better tomorrow."

"Yeah, but this is one special moment. You don't know if you will have tomorrow. This one time, you can do something beautiful and sacrifice a little bit and get out of bed even though it's a little bit cold and say the prayers really carefully."

"Wow, Lord. I'm kind of a selfish guy. I could do something a little unselfish, and I know you are pleased with every little thing, as I would be with my child. I am going to get out of bed this once. It won't kill me once. I am going to say my prayers extra careful, extra-long; in fact, I'm going to say them double. I am going to say them when I am tired."

That shows a little bit of love. This now moment is beautiful. I get to make a little bit of a sacrifice. I get to show God a little extra love. Let go of my selfishness a little bit. I'm going to call on God to bless those I love, bless my church; I'm going to say a Hail Mary slowly and carefully. Thank you, Lord, for the grace of this moment. It's beautiful. This little moment is as right as anything I will ever do in my life. Each small act of love is so precious. Thank You, Lord.

Living in the 'now' moment gives me courage too because sometimes when I fast or something, when Lent comes, I say, "Ah man, forty whole days, I have got to give up my favourite dessert. That's such a long time." I kind of take a negative slant. Wait a minute. I only have to give it up now. It's not so bad. Only this one-day I have to give up dessert. It's beautiful in God's sight.

Look at your life. Do live your life just getting through things and getting them done or living in the now? How do you feel if you perceive that your loved one or friend wants to get your time together finished quickly? Perhaps they keep looking at their watch. Do you treat God that way and rush through your prayers and get them completed rather than being there with God?

26. GOD MOMENTS

Every moment is beautiful. I hope you don't mind one more example from my life.

Every kind of thing that happens, if you live the now, it can be a beautiful, precious experience. It has value, even the simple little things. Sometimes even when you feel dry, even when you don't see the value, in faith, you can know it has a worth.

One time I was in a restaurant, it always seems like when you are in a rush, things don't go according to plan, and I realized I hadn't shaved. I go back and try to shave in a hurry, kind of grumbling, "Why do I have to shave anyway?" The Lord said to me, "Why don't you just embrace the moment? Be at peace. What I want you to do now is just to shave."

I thought, "Why not try it? It won't matter if I'm a wee bit late." So I slowed down and thought, "Lord, I offer you this time of shaving. Thank you, Lord, that I even have a face that I can shave and that I can be at peace with you here for a few moments."

Isn't that a silly thing, just shaving revealed something to me. I remember it still. I had peace. I had a little sense of prayer. I wonder if I could do that every time I shave a little bit. Just feel at peace and do what God gives me now. That's the real secret, not to get through things, but to be there with God in each thing you do.

27. HOW TO SAVE A LOVED ONE

Do you care what happens to your family and your friends?
Do you want to help them and save them from destruction?

I am sure you do. But what do you do to save them and help them? For years I worried about my brother and my parents because they were not going to church or praying or practicing their faith. I prayed for them fairly often, but many times not much. I ask myself if I really loved them that much, for I did very little. I was all caught up with my own life and plans, and enjoyment. I believe my self-concern and self-love captured most of my time and care. Is this real love? Sure I was on the right road and practicing my faith and caring for my salvation. How much did I love them deeply? Yes, I had deep feelings for them, and I thought I loved them, but love is not a feeling, but a decision to really help and do something that would save them.

What did I finally decide to do? Here is my experience. I prayed for the conversion of my parents for over ten years, and I saw no results. I even complained to God that the more I prayed for them, the worse they became. I kept saying to God, "You are my Father, so why do you not answer my prayers?" Why did Jesus promise, "Keep asking, and you will receive?" It is not happening.

I was tempted to quit praying for my parents, but by the grace of God, I persevered. I was a seminarian at the time, and I only got home every two years. To my surprise, my parents had started going back to church on Sundays after ten years' absence. Two years later, when I arrived home, they were saying the rosary every day.

Then they moved to Calgary, and they were near the church, and I nearly fainted with amazement that they were going to daily Mass. A few years later, they moved to Lethbridge, and my father agreed to make a Live-In retreat with my mother, and they enjoyed it and moved even closer to the Lord.

God led me to read my spiritual diary written nearly twenty years before. I had written with doubt that God would ever answer my prayers as the scripture had promised. I expressed with some irritation to Jesus, complaining, "at least, why could you not hear my prayer and get them to go back to church. That is not asking too much, is it, God?"

I broke down weeping when I realized God had answered my prayer more thoroughly than I could have ever dreamed or dared to ask. Jesus did the impossible. My father, at sixty-five years old, was going to prayer meetings and praising God. Then I asked the Lord, "Why did you not answer my prayer sooner? Why did you wait for so many years?"

He spoke to my heart by saying, "Think about it. If I had answered your prayer right away, you would have said thank you, Lord, and then stopped praying. By your continued prayer and struggle of faith, I was able to lead you and deepen my relationship with you. You may not even have remained in the priesthood if it were not for your continuing call to pray for your parents. My delay was to help you and your parents because of my love for all of you.

As I grew in faith and prayed more, I decided to say the rosary every day. I asked others to pray for them. I had Masses offered for them. Most important of all, I prayed much longer and grew in holiness myself. I learned to trust God more and learned about my power to save them by praying the Chaplet of Divine Mercy for them. Even now, fifty years later, I am still praying for them but with more faith, as I know the power that God gives us all to save those we care about, and I make the time to pray by the grace of God.

Now I realize I did not only fail to love them as I could have, but I did not even love myself, as I should. Try to trust that you can genuinely save others and yourself by calling on Jesus's mercy in prayer. Ask Jesus to increase your trust in Him and His promises of great graces for those you pray for and for salvation.

You do have power. If you believe this and you really love others, you will keep praying for them. I understood intellectually in the power of prayer, but I did not pray all that much for my family and loved ones. Then I decided with the grace of God to pray regularly for those I love. I realized that if I cared about somebody and I wanted to get him or her to heaven, I would keep praying for them faithfully. Also, I would stay after them to pray and read about God's love because I know that if they prayed, Jesus would give them the grace they need to seek Him. Then as they persevere in prayer, and in reading the scripture, the love of Jesus could capture their hearts.

We all need prayer, so please pray for me, too, as I pray for you.

28. WHAT HAS CAPTURED YOU?

Are you willing and courageous enough to honestly look at your life and see what has captured your heart and your time, and what is the most important thing that you seek in your life?

What things in your life have captured your time, your heart, and your thoughts? Which has become extremely important to you? Has God, or Jesus, captured your heart, or has the world captured your heart? What we spend our time on is usually what captures our heart. If we spend a reasonable amount of time in prayer and seeking the Lord, He can win our hearts.

Here is a fundamental truth, that almost anything can capture us if we keep going back to it, and getting involved in it, and forming a habit of doing it. I never really liked tennis, but a good friend of mine kept after me, and just to be kind to him, I kept playing even though I would lose, and it wasn't enjoyable at all. But then it finally captured me, and I wanted to play all the time, even every day. It became the most desirable thing in my life.

Some things, such as drugs and alcohol, sexual pleasure, and pornography, can capture us even after having only one or two experiences of the pleasure that we receive. Many of us have psychological wounds, and we did not receive the love and the care that we needed when we were young. Because of this, we are often more vulnerable to be captured by something that fills this emptiness and soothes this pain.

If a young man or woman we're both stranded together on an island, they would most likely capture each other's heart, and they would fall in love with each other. Many of the saints found that the Lord would capture their heart if they went out into the desert alone, and they had no one else to talk to, and spend their time talking to the Lord and seeking Him.

Every human being has an emptiness and a hunger and a great thirst. As I look at my life, and the experience of others, I know, I see that we all try to fill our desires and our emptiness with something. Everything we do is to fulfill some want or desire within us. Sometimes we feel somewhat satisfied and receive pleasure from fulfilling our wants. But it is never enough, and we keep seeking more and more, something that will fill the emptiness in us. Something that gives us pleasure or satisfaction captures nearly all of us. By 'captured,' I mean it has power over us, and we seek it more and more and more.

I see this in my life. Many things in this world have captured me. In my mind, I know I've had enough of this, and I shouldn't be going for more. However, my body and my emotions take over, and I keep seeking it. A simple example of that is sometimes when we eat something we like, and we want another dish full and even another.

People get addicted to drinking, to drugs, to smoking, sexual pleasure, to work, to sports, etcetera. Almost anything can capture us.

Sometimes what captures us is rather good and doesn't harm us except that it takes up all our time and prevents us from other things that perhaps we should be doing. I've been captured to a degree by many, many things. Horseback riding, music, dancing, girlfriends, hobbies, work, mountain climbing, etcetera have captured me, for example. Unfortunately, I must confess that several sinful things have captured me.

Some of the things that captured me have had such a hold on me that I had to struggle for a very long time and pray and get God's special grace to overcome them and let go of them. Think about what has captured you and make a decision about seeking the Lord more and allowing Him to capture your heart.

In the last two years, I have retired and am not able to seek and experienced many of the things I like. My health and the pains I experience limit my ability to enjoy the pleasures of this life. It opened the door for me to seek the Lord more in prayer. He had captured my heart before, but then when dry times came, I spent more time on other things, and they started to capture my time and my life. Whenever I neglected prayer to some degree, other things would come in and capture my heart and life more and more. The Lord would get squeezed out.

At first retirement and separation from worldly things and was very difficult and unsatisfying, but as I worked at spending time with the Lord, it became a great joy, and the Lord gave me an experience of His love and captured my heart more and more.

29. I HAVE BECOME A CHILD AGAIN

Jesus said, "Truly I tell you, whoever does not receive the kingdom of God as a little child will never enter it" (Luke 18:17).

I am becoming as a little child because I'm losing the ability to take care of myself. I'm getting weaker, and it's difficult to walk. I'm going to need someone to take care of me. Some of the older priests now need diapers. And some even need help to change their diapers, and some can no longer wash. It could also happen to me in a year or so. It is very humbling. I believe it can lead me to the truth that without God, I can do nothing. He is my Father and must look after me every moment of my life; and washes me and keeps me clean, and helps me in all that I do, even to eat and to pray.

Without God, I can do nothing, absolutely nothing, not even breathe, or do anything right and holy. I am entirely dependent upon Him. It is a blessing in the end, even though rather painful, to die to myself and to face the truth that every good thing comes from God, and apart from Him, I am nothing but misery, weakness, and sin. So I thank God for my humiliation because it leads me to the truth.

With His help, I can rejoice even in my weakness and my loss of everything so that I seek everything from Him. He loves me, and He alone can take care of me. I ask of you to face this truth and pray for a meek and humble heart. Unless you become as a little child, you cannot enter the kingdom of God.

Jesus said, "Let the little children come to me, and do not stop them; for it is such as these that the kingdom of heaven belongs"(Matthew 19:14). Jesus teaches that to be like children means to be as dependent on Him as little children are dependent on their parents. To live in God's kingdom is to depend on Him for everything.

Therefore, I try to obey Jesus and embrace becoming like a child, dependent on my heavenly Father.

30. FORGIVE EVERYONE

Can you let go of the past and forgive everyone and start anew as if you were never hurt?

I know a lady whose only daughter was kidnapped and raped and killed at nine years of age. The lady was destroyed and angry and filled with hate. She was angry with God, too, for letting this happen to her innocent daughter. How could she trust God, that He was kind and loving if He allowed this to happen when He could have protected this innocent child? She stopped going to church and praying and was angry and bitter.

However, by the grace of God, she could not stand the anger she felt anymore, and she went for help, and finally was able to return to church and to try to pray for guidance. She did the impossible, by the grace of God, and let go of her bitterness toward God. She returned to prayer, and little by little, God was able to show her that her daughter was in heaven in great glory and happiness. She was praying for her mother and waiting for her to come and join her. She had no resentment against her murderer.

To make a long story short, the mother received more grace to do what she describes as utterly impossible for a human being. She visited the murderer in prison and prayed for him, and after many tries won him over to ask for forgiveness, and she forgave him. Then she spent the rest of her life traveling all over the world, telling her story of forgiveness to others who are angry and hurt by injustice and terrible tragedies.

Think about this and pray about it. Pray for those who have anger and have not let go and forgive.

Peter questioned Jesus: "How often must I forgive," my brother? Jesus answered, "seventy times seven times." (Matthew 18:22) We must forgive all who have hurt us infinity times infinity.

The truth is people do not have the power to forgive. As the poet Alexander Pope said, "To err is human; to forgive is divine." Only God can forgive. To forgive, you can decide to accept God's grace to forgive. This grace is always available. Pray for this grace, and do not give up. It takes effort and lots of prayer and surrender.

The best time to forgive is immediate. You must decide for forgiveness right away, even if you do not feel it and want it in your emotions. You do not want to die with unforgiveness in your heart. Jesus will help you, and think how He has forgiven you. You will know that you have forgiven someone when you will show mercy to him or her, even if you do not feel like it; that is, you will treat them better than they deserve.

There is a misunderstanding that forgiveness is condoning the sins of others, but it isn't at all. The Lord has forgiven all our sins and has never condoned any sin. If you feel like you don't want to forgive, pray, and ask the Lord to make you willing to forgive.

31. SURRENDER

Even in the natural human level, we experience joy and
peace when we trust and surrender.

Let us take, for example, a little child who gets hurt.
If the child runs to its mother and throws himself into her
arms in trust, and allows the mother to embrace him, then he
usually feels secure, and the pain is not so overwhelming.
Now everything is okay. I am loved and cared for and safe.
However, the child must have trust and surrender to the love
of its mother.

With God, it is very similar. If we truly trust that He
loves us and has care of us, and we do not waiver, and we
surrender to His love in confidence, then we can have peace
and security. "I do not have to be worried; Jesus is with me
and will bring me through this."

Now we can be very stubborn and cling on to what
we feel we must have, and so be very unhappy because our
heart is set on what we want and not on what God gives us.
To receive the consolation and security of the Lord, we need
to surrender to His love and care and let go of our plan. It is
especially true if what we want is sinful and contrary to the
will of God.

If we will let go of what we must have and surrender
to what the Lord has given us, and turn to Jesus trusting in
His love and care, as soon as we surrender Jesus in His
mercy says to us, this day of your repentance and trust, my
salvation comes to you and you have heaven inside of you.

I do not always 'feel' the trust, but I keep constantly praying this way, "Jesus, I decided to trust in you even in the darkness. Jesus, the desire of my heart, is to trust completely in your great love for me. Help me to love you in return." I pray you surrender and continuously pray for more trust and love.

32. A VERY IMPORTANT TRUTH
Suffering tears us open...

When life is hard and painful, and we are suffering, we are torn open, and the hole can receive great gifts from God, and we become able to help others in more significant ways. I believe God invites us to gaze upon the image of the crucified to soften our hearts toward God, and to know that God's heart is always softened toward us, even and most especially in our suffering.

It is the mystery of suffering and the Christian revelation that the place of the wound is the place of the most significant gain and gift. It is the mystery of the "cross and resurrection," revealing that our very wounds can become redemptive wounds if we trust in God and surrender. Strange that an innocent, unjustly wounded man became the salvation of the world. The cross, an instrument of torture and suffering, is the symbol of hope and salvation for all of Christianity. The brutal killing of God becomes the salvation of the world. This mysterious truth revealed; that the very worst things have the power to become the very best things. Nothing, no matter how bad, needs to be permanently destructive. Absolutely everything is capable of leading to life and happiness.

Now looking to the wounded one and accepting our wounds and everybody else's wounds too save us. Our lives are grounded in humble weakness instead of any need to have power or pride in our strength and success. Even great people have wounds and vulnerabilities. St. Paul himself, humbly admitted that God had given him a "thorn in the flesh, an angel of Satan to buffet me" (2 Corinthians 12:7), which he says was necessary "to keep me from getting too proud."

In most people I know, their goodness comes from the struggle with their wound and weakness. All of us must daily recognize our imperfection and sin, or we become proud and arrogant and tend to be critical or look down on others. Either you embrace the pain within yourself, or it is a stumbling block and festering wound. You can only do this by the ever-available grace of God.

Jesus' wounded body is a sign of what we are all doing to one another and the world by our sins. Jesus transformed His sufferings into healing for the world. He will help us to do the same as we embrace our sufferings and unite them with His for the salvation of the world. Jesus' resurrected body is a sign and a proof of God's promise of victory over all suffering, tragedy, and death for all of us as we come into union with Him.

The two images suffering and death AND resurrection and eternal life, are a picture of all of human life.

33. FOR ALL OF YOU WHO ARE GOOD

This reflection is for all of us who feel we are 'pretty good guys' and doing very well in the sight of God. Perhaps we will be blessed and learn some truth.

Here is a little joke that has a point to it: Once there were two Devils, an older one and the new, young devil. They went out to the world to tempt everybody. They were tempting everyone to commit adultery, to gossip, to lie, to steal, to be lazy, to cheat, etc. etc. However, there was one lady, faithful to her prayers, attending Mass faithfully whom they never tempted.

The younger devil said to the older: "We are called to tempt that lady, and you're not doing your job. I may have to report you to Satan, the king of devils because you're not tempting her."

The older devil says, "You are young and inexperienced. What if we tempted her, and she fell into some big sin? You might think that is good, but I look deeper. If she fell, she might have to humble herself and then would repent and go to confession, and would end up knowing the truth that she needs God, that all of her goodness is a gift from God, and so we would lose her."

The younger devil said, "What do you mean? We've already lost her. Look how she says her prayers and stays out of all sin."

The other devil says, "Look more deeply, see how proud she is? She thinks she's better than everyone else. She has pride, and so we already have her, so we don't want to tempt her because then she would have to face the truth and humble herself, and truly be close to God."

The whole point of this story is to be careful of pride and to know that any goodness we have is a gift from God. To judge others and condemn others makes one like the Pharisees. Look carefully at the parable of the Pharisee. At the front of the church he says, "I thank God I'm better than the rest of men; better than that publican there at the back." But the publican, not daring to look up to heaven, bowed his head and said, "Have mercy on me, a sinner."

Then Jesus says, "the publican went out of the church, justified in the sight of God, whereas the Pharisee, filled with pride, was not pleasing in the sight of God." (Luke 18:13)

Pray continually for the gift of humility. Say many times, "Jesus meek and humble of heart, make my heart like unto thine."

I pray that at least when I see my pride. I can humble myself and say, "I am the worst of sinners, filled with pride. Lord have mercy on me, a sinful and proud man."

Let us pray for each other, for I am a sinner, and we are all sinners, and we all need the mercy of God. The only thing we can claim apart from God is our sinfulness. Jesus says, "Everything good comes from God. Every perfect gift is from Him" (James 1:17).

Without Him, we can do nothing but sin, but in Him, we can be holy and beautiful and do all things, as we humble ourselves. It is essential to know we are holy and righteous to an extent, and there is much beautiful goodness in us, as well as some weaknesses. We can rejoice and thank God for the good part, and not be all down on ourselves; and at the same time, humbly admit it is all God in us, and not us. We are not better than anyone else.

St. Augustine says, the three most important virtues are, humility, humility, and humility. But should we not say, "No, it should be faith, hope, and love, not humility?"

The answer is that St. Augustine saw the truth, that if we have humility, then God can give us all the other virtues, which are more important. But we cannot receive them from God if we are proud and do not have humility. Think of Mary, the Mother of God. She was utterly holy. She faced the truth and said, "He looks upon the lowliness of his servant girl, and He who is mighty has done great things for me." (Luke 1:48)

Mary faces that She did not do it herself; and that it is all a gift from God. She was the holiest because She was the most humble and faced the love and truth, that apart from God, she was nothing. The saints say that to think yourself better than someone else will do you a lot of harm, whereas to judge yourself, the least will open you to great graces and blessings.

You can judge the actions of another person as wrong, but you do not know what grace the other person has, and what wounds they have experienced. If you were in their shoes and had their grace and trials, you might have done much worse; and if they had the grace that you have, they might have been much closer to God than you are. Jesus said, "Judge not, and you will not be judged."

We should say, as the saints said of themselves when they saw a poor sinner, "There, but for the grace of God, go I."

I am a sinner. Lord have mercy (I know you do). Yes, Lord, there is good in me, which is from you and not me. I am sinful and weak, and I need God's mercy and help and forgiveness always. Anything kind and loving in me is from Him and because of His merciful presence within me. I cannot even pray or believe or love or stay out of sin without the help of my Lord and saviour. He is always there to help me and lift me up.

34. PARODICAL CHILDREN

Here is a true story that I experienced...

I came to know this man, who had gotten angry with his parents and ran away at the age of six. Somehow he got to a big city that was nearby, and a gang member who was involved in the mafia picked him up and sort of kidnapped him. He fed him and clothed him and used him to beg for money and then taught him how to pickpocket on the street. As he got older, they gave him a gun, and he was involved in robberies for the gang. He was a very talented young man and had leadership qualities, and so he ended up as one of the leaders in the mafia. He had access to lots of money, as he became a leader in the labour union in Chicago.

To make a long story short, somehow years later, he met a young lady who was a Catholic and was very strong in her faith and her character and relationships. He was very impressed with her and her strength of character. He married her and went against some of the mafia rules, and so, they escaped and moved out west to Alberta. I met them there, and he was open to instruction in the Catholic faith. He had quite a conversion and came to know Jesus.

He was like the Prodigal Son who ran away from home, then came back to his father, his heavenly Father. He was starving spiritually, and by the grace of God, realized he needed his spiritual Father and his spiritual mother, Mary.

Getting to know him and his story had a deep impression on me. I saw in his experience the story of the Prodigal Son who ran away from his father and mother, and then repented and came back to his family.

For all of us, our true family from whom we received existence is God's family. He created us and gave us life. Perhaps we sort of run away from God and go on our own and get into sin and need to come back to our heavenly Father. I pray that we could all see that we are prodigal children and must return more fully to our spiritual mother and Father, for our soul, and our very existence comes from God, and it was He who knit us together in our earthly mother's womb.

Some people use God's name in vain and dishonour Him. They do not spend as much time with God as they do their earthly father. They do not think about God as much as they do their earthly father. They do not realize that they still need their heavenly Father. He still has to keep them alive by His love and care.

One little child I knew used to pray to God to care for his father and mother and brother and sister and then say, "Yes, and God take good care of yourself for if anything happens to you, we will all be in trouble! We need you, God."

That child had wisdom! May we have wisdom about our need to be very close to God.

35. BEAUTIFUL DISASTERS

I'll tell you a story about embracing painful, kind of disastrous things.

I was at The Way of Holiness Retreat Centre in Alberta, and this couple that was getting married had come to visit me. They wanted to pray and prepare for their wedding. We went for a little walk and went down on the side of a kind of a cliff, and there were different ledges, and we went out on a ledge. It was the beautiful scenery of the Athabasca River below.

Mark, the husband-to-be, said, "I'm going to take a picture of you and Amanda. Just stand over there, it's a good background. Move down a little bit." We were right on the edge of this cliff. "Just move over a little bit more as that's an even better background."

Mark goes to take the picture, and BANG something hits me in the head. I feel like my whole head has caved in, and blood is pouring down my face, and I'm kind of collapsing. I'm down on the ground. I'm dying. I'm bleeding; blood is flowing all over my head and into my eyes and onto my shirt. What happened? Something hit me! Something hit me!

To make a long story short, they are mopping up the blood with handkerchiefs and looking at the cut. It's just above my eye. I come around and say I've got a cell phone, call 911, and maybe they can save me.

At that point, I thought I was dying, but at the same time, I thought it couldn't be that bad because I'm conscious, and I'm thinking reasonably clearly. They phone 911. The ambulance comes, and the rescue group comes. They finally find me, and they get me on a stretcher, and they are carrying me up the cliff, which is very painful as they thought I had a broken neck. They strapped me down, and that was even more painful. But the whole point of the thing was that it was a highlight. I just embraced it with God's grace. In the hospital, it was good. God brought great good out of it.

Later we found out that there were some young people up higher on another ledge, and they threw something heavy, a rock or something, and it hit me in the head, and I just happened to be in that spot. They couldn't see us down below. They just threw a rock, no harm intended. They ran away when they saw my friend come up, all covered with blood to get the ambulance people.

I thank God for it all, even though at first I complained and thought, "I ended up right in the spot where this rock was going to come, and you knew it all. Why didn't you protect me?"

But then I thought, "No, everything that happens He is there. He didn't cause the rock directly to come, He didn't particularly want it to come, but He allows us to be in the world where things can happen. He doesn't always stop everything, but He's there to bring good out of it, a greater good."

So I thanked Him. "Thank you, Lord, for that experience, thank you that I could turn to you, what a beautiful thing. I could have just been 'Oh what a disaster, ended up in the hospital in pain, did permanent brain damage' but I say no, I give it all to you. I trust you, Lord. If I die, I die. If there's permanent damage, there's permanent damage. You love me, and you will bring good out of it, whatever happens."

I had great peace and joy even in the pain.

36. HOPE

The virtue of hope is not just a wish, but a certainty, because of the promise of God and our faith that He keeps His promises.

How does a person keep hoping and trusting amid trials and persecutions? How can we have the courage to face suffering and death? Because of our trust, we can rejoice even in the worst situations and consider it a privilege to suffer for Jesus' sake? "By faith and trust, we were saved" (Romans 8:24).

It is not always true that hope springs eternal in the human breast. There are suicides, addictions, and human weakness and psychological wounds, which often lead to despair, not hope. Real and lasting hope is not humanly possible. God must give hope.

In Ephesians 1:18, it says that "God enlightens our innermost vision that we may know the great hope to which He has called us."

This hope will not leave us disappointed because the love of God has poured out into our hearts through the Holy Spirit, Who is with us. Let us pray that God, the source of hope, will fill us with all joy and peace through our trust in Him.

We need to keep proclaiming the truth that God loves us and wants our happiness and will always be there for us in His great mercy and love. Let us pray that all our suffering will lead to endurance and the strength to trust that all things will work for the good for those who believe in God. The more we pray and read and proclaim the truth, the more profound will our trust becomes and our confidence in His never-failing love and mercy.

37. DEALING WITH PAIN AND SUFFERING

Life can be painful when we have deep wounds.

Here are some thoughts to help you to get through painful feelings and sadness:
First, try to live just the now. Pretend you were just born, and the past was just a dream, and you only have fifteen minutes to live and then go to heaven, and God wants you just to live the few minutes you have and try to enjoy it for Him. Take, for example, eating your meal, think, "All I need to do now is taste my food and try to enjoy it and try not to think about anything else. Life is now. I have food, and most of the world are hungry and have no food, or very little, and poor food at that. Thank you, Lord, I have food; most do not. It tastes pretty good."

Try to do it for five minutes, and you will feel a little less of the pain, as long as you focus on the food.
Here are some other suggestions to try:

• Pray for someone you know with great suffering; trust that you blessed the person.

• Watch a few minutes of interesting TV or something humorous. It can help.

• Sing a joyful song out loud to the Lord is also very helpful.

• Phone someone and talk to him or her and think about that person. Is it a little less pain, at least when you were thinking about that person?

- Say to the Lord over and over again, "Jesus, I trust in you to bring me through this trial and struggle."

- Thank God that at the end of your journey, you will die and go to heaven, and all pain will be gone, and you will have infinite joy that you do not deserve. Try to imagine it as vividly as you can, entering heaven. Think of the glory of heaven. Reading and proclaiming the truth of the beauty of heaven can bless you and all for whom you pray.

Let me know if any of this worked for you. Pray before you try each thing. I am praying for you. Think of me. I am often in constant pain and have peace, at least when I get my mind distracted by something other than my pain.

38. BE A LIGHT TO THE WORLD

What was it that gave life to the world and saved all of us from eternal death?

It was Jesus, who emptied himself of his power and glory and his glorious life in heaven, to become one of us. He became a weak little child, having no power, or majesty, or glory. Then he even emptied himself of his human life and dignity, and was whipped and spit upon, and mocked and crucified and died.

But it was through this death to himself, and his weakness and his humiliation and his suffering, that he gave life to the world. I pray that you and I will have the courage to take up our cross and die to self, and follow Jesus, and be a light for the world with Jesus.

All of the saints had a kind of power from their union with God. This power is still there in their message for the world. They got this power by letting go of all fear of suffering, all need for self-power, prestige, and possessions. They let go of any need for their small self to be influential; and came to know who they were in God, and thus who they really are as beloved children of God; and of their nothingness apart from God.

The saints emptied themselves and lost everything and took up their cross and followed Jesus. The ability to change and heal people is the fruit of suffering, and various forms of death to self, since the false self does not surrender without a fight. Suffering forces us to not be in control. It takes away our power and opens the door to God's power and His plan for our life.

Some form of suffering is necessary to teach us how to live, not in the false idea of our control, but to give that control back to God. Then we become instruments for God and not for ourselves.

The saints voluntarily leaped into the pain of death to self, from which most of us are trying to escape. They put total trust in Jesus' way of the cross and His love for us. By God's grace, they could see the eventual passing of all things, and their passing away. They did not wait for salvation later after death but grasped it here and now for themselves, and even more for others.

They were a light for the world by uniting their suffering with the suffering of Jesus and offering themselves as a sacrifice to the Lord, for the salvation of the world.

39. THE MYSTERY OF SUFFERING

If God is good, why does He allow suffering? Couldn't God create a perfect world?

Couldn't God have created a world where there was no sickness or suffering, where everything went well? It's a strange mystery. Why did God allow all this suffering and pain?

God is looking for true love. I think true, deep, freely given love is necessary for our happiness. I think there's some mysterious thing that to love, you have to have the freedom not to love. You can see it a little bit if you were going to get married, and you really loved this person, so you said," I love them so much I'm just going to make them love me because I'm afraid they might not. They won't have any choice; they'll have to love me."

That destroys love if you have to make somebody love. If they freely choose to love when they could choose not to, there's something beautiful and glorious about that. If they want to love you, even though it cost quite a bit and they have to sacrifice to love you, somehow it's even more beautiful. God gave us that freedom, and with that freedom, people can get hurt. We can choose not to love, we can choose to reject, we can choose to hurt somebody, we can choose to steal, and we can choose to commit adultery. We can also choose to be heroic and to love even when something is tempting us not to. There's something beautiful about this sacrificial love, free choice.

We can see it a little bit in this little thing. If I said to you, "I really love you. I love you a lot. I want to help you. I want to do something good for you, something great. Do you know what I'm going to do for you? I'm going to eat my favourite chocolate cake for you. That's how much I love you!"

You would laugh and say come on Father Clair. That doesn't show love just because you eat your favourite chocolate cake for me. What if I said, "Okay I love you so I won't eat my chocolate cake? I won't have any chocolate cake for a month. I won't have any dessert for a month. I'll even fast for a month. In fact, I'll even pray for you and make time for prayer, fast and, give up all desserts. I want to be a blessing for you because I love you. I will even pay your debt. I hear you're in debt for $50,000.00. I'll sacrifice, I'll work hard, I'll save that money, and I'll pay off your debt. Is that love? I'll do it even if I get nothing in return. I'll do it just for you."

Can you see that somehow in some mysterious way, love is tied in with sacrifice and suffering? Sacrifice is a little bit hard, and somehow that's beautiful. It's beautiful when someone will go through trials and struggles and suffering for love of you.

Think of all the movies we watch, books we read, and all the TV shows we see about a hero. I don't think we would admire a hero who never suffers, never has struggles, never has difficulties or pain. He just goes through, and everything is excellent. He helps everybody, but it doesn't cost him a thing. He doesn't have to struggle or work hard at it.

It doesn't somehow inspire us. It's not the kind of story that would be popular. I watch all the stories and all the popular movies. It's usually about somebody that has to go through a lot of pain, and they finally have victory. That's what we admire.

There's a beauty about struggle and going through pain, sacrifice, and suffering and coming through it with joy. We love those beautiful stories. God loves those beautiful stories. He gives us all a chance to be a hero. We like heroic love. Do you want someone to love you just mediocre? Do they never have to pay a big price? Do they never have to do anything hard for you? Would you instead wish that someone loves you heroically, that they would do anything for you, even lay down their life for you? There's that mystery of free will that is needed and that God wants heroic love, and He gives us a chance to be heroic in our love.

We've got to remember this critical point. You don't have to do it all by yourself. God's strength is there. His help is there. He gives you that power to love heroically. Jesus heroically loved. Mary got that power from God. The saints got that power from God. They weren't praying and saying, "Oh, why do I have to go through all of this? It is too much. God, this isn't fair. Why do I have to go through all this suffering to love you, to be a saint? I don't like it, it's terrible."

Read the lives of the saints. They have joy in that heroic love. The scripture says there's joy in love. There's joy in sacrifice. I know even young people who have done things heroic, who have walked miles through the snow to rescue somebody. They say, "I never felt so good in my life."

I said, "you nearly froze your feet; wasn't that painful?" They never counted the cost of sacrifice and were willing to forget about themselves completely.

"You had nothing to eat, and you walked all that way?" They said, "Yes, but I felt good inside because I was doing something beautiful. I was loving somebody. I was helping somebody, and I felt good inside."

People feel good when they heroically embrace a trial, difficulty, or pain for the love of God and the love of others. God is there to give them that courage. It's a mystery again. I can't explain it all. Maybe you could see a little glimpse of it, that it's a beautiful world when people can be heroic. I believe that God gives everybody that grace. I think even in cases when somebody is overwhelmed by all his or her suffering and trial as I was as a little child, we can look back and say thank you, God. Through that suffering and being overwhelmed, it expanded my heart and gave me compassion for others who are suffering. It gave me some humility and helped me to be capable of love, capable of understanding Jesus' suffering. It helped me respond to other people's pain.

I believe that at the time we feel, 'this is too much,' God is there for us. Here's what I think. You have to decide what you believe. I believe that if you surrender to God, trust Him, open your heart to Him, and look to Him for strength, He brings you through it with power. Sure, you suffered but read what the saints say. They love the suffering. They long for it. They say it's the heart of life. They see it expands their heart, and they learn to love. They're more capable of joy.

I think when we surrender and we let the Lord's grace come, and we trust God, we can go through the suffering with strength. They put St. Lawrence on a hot griddle, like barbecuing somebody, and they're burning his back. God gave him so much strength; he was able to joke and say, "Oh, I think I'm done on that side; you can turn me over."

I think God will give us incredible strength if He allows us to have big sufferings. If we turn to Him, if we surrender, if we trust Him, He will give us the grace to get through our trials. It's still a mystery, but I believe even people who are overwhelmed with their suffering and don't do so well, that God's there for them. He brings them through it, and He wipes away their tears. At least that's what God did for me, even when I was overwhelmed. I think He loves everybody. I trust in Him. It doesn't make sense that He's not loving,

I believe the glory and the reward and the joy of learning to love through sacrifice leads to such happiness that we would say, "That suffering was nothing compared with the joy I have now forever and ever and ever and ever!"

I bet you, all of us would go through a minute of intense suffering for five days of great joy. We might even go through an hour of suffering for a year of great joy. We might even be willing to go through a week of suffering for ten years of great joy. We might even be ready to go through a month of suffering for a lifetime of great happiness. Are we willing to go through an instant of suffering for an eternity of great joy? Are we willing to do that? I think with God's grace, we can.

I think if we had a soft, soft life and we didn't go through much suffering, it would be hard to be loving, hard to be very noble. I don't think we would be capable of great love. If you're not capable of great love, then you're not capable of a great union. If you marry somebody, and they're not capable of loving you very much, how can you be genuinely one with them, especially if you love them greatly? We would all like to marry somebody that loves us with powerful love, someone who would even be willing to lay down his or her life for us. I heard a man talking, and he said, "For my children, I would stand in front of a Mac truck even if it squashed me! For my wife, I would fight a tiger to save her!"

He seemed to be willing to suffer. The heart of it is, God made us for heroic love. There's something there, some mystery. Jesus loves us heroically. He suffered and went through great pain to save us.

God is not dumb. He makes this world glorious. Anyone who wants to turn to Him, surrender to Him, get strength from Him will be glorious. They will have the strength to go through their pain. They can even have joy in their trials and sufferings as the saints did. I believe that grace is there for all of us to be heroic, to be courageous, and to have a great reward.

40. DEATH IN MY FAMILY

I just got back from a funeral, and I want to thank all of you for your prayers.

I am very close to my only sister Dorothy. It is her husband, Alex, who died, and it is most painful for her that her husband of over forty years is gone. I find it challenging to face death when it hits home. I believe that we all tend to avoid thinking about death. We all tend to get caught up with this life as if it were going to last forever; we think little about where we will be after we die.

This life is like one year compared with the hundreds and hundreds of years that will be after we die. When you look back at it and think about it, this life is very, very brief. Compare it with forever and ever, which is more important, where we will be forever and ever or the brief time that we spend in this world?

I know that this life is like life in the womb, which is only nine months. However, those nine months are very, very important as a preparation for the fuller life that comes after we leave our life in the womb. And so, our life in this world is critical to prepare for eternal life. If in the womb we did not get our hands prepared, and our feet prepared, and our mind matured, and our body complete, ready for life after birth, then life after birth might be painful.

I pray that none of us will be unprepared and lose out on the life that Jesus promised. He promised He would raise us from the dead and give us a whole new life. I look forward to being reunited with everyone in the next life in heaven.

We will all have to face death one day, and it could come at any time. It often happens when we least expect, and many of us have had someone we love die suddenly in an accident or a sudden heart attack or sickness. Scripture tells us always to prepare because we do not know the day or the hour. I like to prepare for death every night before I go to bed by praying to Jesus, who alone can raise us from the dead.

I ask people (and you right now), "Who are you?" They say, "What do you mean? I am me," and say their name.

I answer, "You are a son or daughter of the most-high God."

Sometimes I ask, "How long will you live?" They say, "I do not know, probably seventy or so years." No one says, "I will live forever."

I ask them, "Then what happens to you?" I get various answers such as, I will die, or I do not know, or how should I know for sure."

I tell people if you give your life to Jesus, you will never really die but go to heaven. Jesus will raise you from death. He will provide you with the fullness of life and happiness forever. You can have the fulfillment of every desire greater than you can ever dream. Scripture says, "Eye cannot see, nor ear cannot hear, nor can you even imagine what great things God has prepared for those who love Him." (1Corinthians 2:9)

Jesus is the only human being in history who predicted He would rise from the dead and who promised us He would raise us from the dead if we trusted in Him and followed Him.

Even if I wondered if all of this may not be true, I still would try to pray and trust in Jesus because even if it were not true, I would have nothing to lose, and if it were true, I would lose everything by not praying or trusting in Jesus and God.

When I was young, I did not even fully believe in germs until I saw them through a microscope. However, I sort of had trust in what others told me because if they were right, I thought I had best keep clean and wash my hands before eating. I did the same with God and Jesus. I tried to do what others and the saints and the Bible said. I trusted and tried to live a good life and pray. I found it very painful when I failed to love God and others as I should or fell into sin. My refuge and healing came from trusting in the great compassion and mercy that comes through Jesus as He came to call sinners. It gives me strength and consolation. God answered my prayers and gave me faith and later even let me see that He was real and that He has a great love for me. Jesus wants me in heaven so much that He came to earth to rescue me and suffered and died on the cross to save me.

Now I keep praying that God would help others to do as He did for me when I prayed. I do not want anyone to be lost.

41. HOW TO LET GO OF ANXIETY

The peace that surpasses all understanding....

"Have no anxiety about anything, but in everything by prayer and supplication with thanksgiving, let your requests be made known to God. And the peace of God, which passes all understanding, will keep your hearts and your mind safe in Christ Jesus." (Philippians 4:6-7)
We all have stress in our lives. I am sure we have all had anxiety, or still can suffer from anxiety from time to time. When we realize that we are stressed and feel burdened, it is hard to automatically just give it to God at times. We like to carry our burdens, and sometimes even sit in our misery before we can let go.

I know from personal experience that when I hand it over to God right away, I do feel a lot better than when I sit in my misery. There is a peace that follows that right decision to let go and let God carry my burden. Letting go is a tough thing to do, but with the help of the Holy Spirit, we can let go and find freedom.

Try not to listen to your emotions as they lie to you. You may feel that God does not love you or that you are hopeless, or any one of many, many negative things. Feelings can be powerful. However, they can change with the wind, and they do not tell us the truth.
Just because we feel God is unfair or He is fed up with us does not mean it is accurate and the same with what we 'feel' about ourselves. Satan even uses our emotions to discourage us and to lie to us. "The devil is a liar, and the father of lies" (John8:44).

It is a battle to keep renouncing the lies and to keep proclaiming the truth but gradually, we defeat the lies, and they lose their strength. When the feelings come on strong, try to look at it as an opportunity to renounce them and choose to proclaim the truth. Jesus loves you and will bring good and victory out of the struggle.

We get to say and choose. I choose the truth. Jesus is the truth of God's love for me and His victory in my life over my feelings and my wounds.

Dear Jesus, I pray for all of us that struggle with anxiety, that you could give us the strength to keep trusting in you, and handing over our struggles to you each day. We can feel a deep peace when we surrender our hurts and struggles into your hands.

Jesus, we trust in you, Amen.

42. MY LIFE'S GREATEST EXPERIENCE

I believe this is one of the most intense happenings of my whole life.

It happened while I was driving on the long, empty highway in Alberta between Lethbridge and Calgary. I was going down to Lethbridge to give a conference. I was praying while I was driving, and I began to see that the Lord was showing me my whole life. All of a sudden, the Lord showed me all my selfishness. I exclaimed, "Oh no, look at what I have been doing. I have been living for myself, not bearing fruit really, not living for others or God, but just doing my own will and what I like doing! Oh, look at my selfishness."

My life was more for me because I got fun out of it. I wanted to be this great honest person, but I could see I was nothing but misery and selfishness. I gave in to anger and all kinds of things. I started crying. I had this dream, and it was all falling apart. I thought that I was doing so well, and I could see I was not. I had to pull off the road because, through the tears, I could not see to drive.

I put my head down on the steering wheel, saying to myself, "Look at me a selfish, sinful man, and here I am a priest. I should have been somebody like a saint, beautiful and great."

I wanted it to be that way, but I saw how I'd failed, and all my sin and weakness. I cried out that I wanted to be a good person and do what is right, and my whole life has been a failure. I had not done what I should have. I did not become what God called me to be. I'd ultimately failed to be the person and the priest that I should have been.

I was utterly overwhelmed, and I fell on my face on the seat of my car. My face was twisting in pain, and I was crying from somewhere deep in my heart. When I opened my eyes, I couldn't see anything. It was like I was blind. I cried out again and again to the Lord that I wanted to be a good person and that I had ruined everything.

After a long time of pain and weeping, I sensed the Lord saying to me that he could help me. He would forgive me and give me a whole new start in life. He kept inviting me to let go of my dream of me being a successful, good, holy person.

The Lord spoke to me and said, "I can redeem it all if you trust in my mercy and surrender. I can give you true greatness. You can't make yourself great."

I replied, "But I want to be great on my own. Now that I have messed up everything how, can I ever be anything admirable? My dream for my life will never come true!"

God said, "Surrender and trust in my mercy."

I finally said, "Lord, okay. It is hard but, I surrender. I am not great but, you can make me great. All goodness and everything is yours, and I am nothing apart from you. All I have is your love and mercy, and that is enough."

It was a big struggle to put aside my pride and my thinking that I had succeeded, or that I did well and made myself a perfect, successful person. I had to let go of everything I wanted for my life and let everything depend on the mercy and gift of God.

I said my prayer of surrender. Then everything changed, and peace came into my heart. I had a new joy and freedom. My sight came back to me. I was able to see everything again. Everything had changed and turned into a beautiful Technicolor whereas before it all had been so ordinary, sort of black and whites with no real colour or beauty. It was amazing. I lifted my head, my face still twisted, but everything looked different. I can remember even the steering wheel looked beautiful. It is hard to describe.

I looked at the trees and the grass at the side of the road. I gazed at the sky and the clouds. Everything was beautiful! It was like a whole new beautiful world that was given to me by God, not by my effort. Jesus was my peace, my goodness, my strength, and my hope. Everything was God's gift to me.

This experience taught me a great lesson. I have to keep repeating it regularly, even when everything feels dry and not colourful at all. Almost every day, I fail and don't live the day as well as I should have. I get down on myself, then I have to trust the Lord again and surrender and thank Him that everything depends on His mercy.

I think this is the greatest lesson I've ever learned. That the heart of life is the struggle to live the truth; that we can do nothing good or loving or really lasting, without the grace and help of God. We human beings always seem to try to live our life, and be good and successful by our own efforts. It is challenging to realize and accept our dependence on God. Our complete dependence on the mercy and grace of God is the truth that underlies human life and all human goodness.

I pray that this may help you in your life struggle and that you see more and more our need for the constant grace and help of God. Even when we are living a reasonably good life in our eyes, and others tell us we are doing so well, there is truth in this. There can be a great deal of selfishness and pride in what we do. There is also much failure to really love God and others.

43. MY TRIALS

I have been having some severe health problems and suffering recently.

My trials seem huge at times, but the Lord shows me that my troubles are so small compared with most of the people of the world. I tend to be very cowardly as I have had a soft life for eighty-six years. In this time of trial, the Lord speaks to me through the following scripture passages; "Many are the troubles of the just man, but out of them all the Lord delivers him." (Psalm 34:20)

Our trials, rather than being wasted time, and experiences that keep us from being fruitful for Jesus, are a means to purify us and make us more fruitful disciples. "There is cause for rejoicing here. You may for a time have to suffer the distress of many trials; but this is so that your faith, which is more precious than the passing splendor of fire-tried gold, may by its genuineness lead to praise, glory, and honour when Jesus Christ appears" (1Peter 1:6-7). Our suffering and trials are helping us to grow in radical trust in Jesus. It may be difficult to see this at the time of our suffering. "My brothers, count it pure joy when you are involved in every sort of trial. Realize that when your faith is tested, this makes for endurance" (James 1:2-3). "When you come to serve the Lord, prepare yourself for trials. For in fire, gold is tested, and worthy men in the crucible of humiliation" (Sirach 2:1, 5).

"No test has been sent you that does not come to all men. Besides, God keeps his promise. He will not let you be tested beyond your strength. Along with the test, he will give you a way out of it so that you may be able to endure it" (1Corinthians 10:13). I write this with my love and prayers for you, and I ask for your prayers for myself, and those who are suffering. We all need prayer.

44. GRATITUDE

What would you want from someone that you did everything for?

What if you paid someone's debts, took their jail sentence, forgave them one thousand times for all of the hurts they caused you, gave them life, paid a great price to nurse them back to health, healed them, gave them food when they were hungry, and finally died on the cross for the person so that they could be happy with you forever in the beautiful home that you had prepared for them in your castle on the high mountain? What would you expect from them? Would you not want them to be very grateful and to make time to express their thanks and gratitude to you? Perhaps you would even want the person to love you if you did all of this for the love of this person.

Do you thank God for all He had done for you? Or do you complain because you want more and expect more? You have everything and eternal happiness in Heaven beyond your imagination.

Make time to thank the Lord for all his love and for what He has done for you. Create a list of all the good things you have received. Include eyes to see, for music and the beauty of creation; for the food, you eat when most people in the world have nothing; for the truth you have and that you know about Heaven and the truth about God's love for you; for His forgiveness for all of your sins; for His mercy and compassion for you; that you have a bed and a house when many do not; for life and every good thing you ever have had and for my little reminder to be thankful (ha ha).

May the Lord bless you and give you a grateful heart! Make time to thank Him for everything in your life and give Him your love. He loves you with an individual and infinite love that He has for no one else, and your thanks give Him joy!

45. SADIE

A wonderful parable of Jesus's love for us!

Once upon a time, there was a mighty king who lived in a magnificent castle on a mountaintop. One day he called his only son into the throne room and said, "My beloved son, I want you to go down into the city for I have picked out a bride for you. Her name is Sadie. I want you to see if you can win her heart. I warn you that she's in a bit of trouble. Will you go?"

The son happily agreed and set off down the mountainside. As he entered the city, he started asking people, "I'm looking for Sadie. I want her to be my bride." And people would just laugh. He didn't understand. He went a little deeper into the city. "Do any of you know Sadie?" he asked.

And they just kept laughing as they said, "Oh, we know Sadie.

"Well, why are you laughing?" he asked them. And he could never get an answer, just more laughter.

Finally, one person said, "Don't you know why we are laughing? Sadie is a prostitute. She is a disgraceful woman. And you want her as your wife! You look like a great prince and should have a more eligible bride. Besides that, if you find her and marry her, you have to pay her debts. That's the rule of the city. Everything she has, including all her shame and debt, will come upon you. Do you understand that?"

At first, the prince looked a little dismayed, but then he said, "Well, I guess that makes sense. If I marry her, I will be responsible for everything she did and have to pay her debts. But I am rich, and I'm willing to do that. However, look at it the other way. Did you know I am the prince? So if Sadie marries me, even though I have to pay her debts, she will become the princess. If she's willing to come, there will be a fabulous celebration in the castle when I bring her home as my bride. My father will heal her and transform her. I am still going to find her and woo her."

Now when he found Sadie, it was worse than he thought. Not only did she have significant debts, but she had also committed crimes, meaning she would be beaten as well as imprisoned, perhaps even executed. As the stranger had warned him, if he married Sadie, he would be liable for all her debts and share in all the disgrace and punishment due to her. But his love for her was great, so he continued to pursue Sadie. He was willing to make full reparations for her wrongdoings. But the question remains: will Sadie say yes? Will she realize her need? Will she accept the prince's love and allow him to save her from suffering?

Well, it's not too hard to figure out the meaning of the parable. Jesus is the prince who came down to earth to pursue humanity and pay the debt of our sins that we might be transformed and join Him and God the Father in heaven.

Will you say yes to his proposal of union and give yourself to Him and stick with Him in good times or bad, in sickness or health, rich or poor until death unites you with Him and you are taken to the castle to live happily forever sharing His very life and glory?

I believe it's a profound parable that gets at the very heart of Christianity because no one can come to the Father except through deep, physical, and spiritual union with Jesus. But just as Sadie couldn't be forced to go with the prince to enter the castle and had to choose to follow him, we are faced with our own choice to follow Jesus. What do you say? Do you believe in Jesus as your Lord and Saviour, as the one who loves you like a bridegroom? In scripture, it means that God is the bridegroom, and the whole Church, each one of us, is His bride. It's symbolic talk, but there's a truth hidden here.

The choice is yours. Either you say 'no' to union with Him, or you say 'yes' to union with Him. You face this choice every day. If you are one with Him in this life, you will be one with Him in heaven and share in His glory. He takes on all our sin, and gives us a share in His glory, all because He loves us.

One final thing: repentance and reconciliation can reunite us with Jesus whenever we make a mistake. If we repent, the Lord redeems us again, and restores everything. It's an incredible mystery of love. He never gives up on us. Don't miss out on the opportunity to return to Jesus. Never forget that God picked each of you out from all eternity and decided to love you into life. And He still loves you, no matter if you are the worst sinner in the world. He loves you, and He keeps seeking you.

Meditate upon this mystery, the endless pursuit of God for each of us.

46. THEOLOGY OF THE PRESENT MOMENT

This message is the most critical and most life-changing that I found in all the years of living! Please make time to read it carefully and prayerfully.

If you think about it, all there is to life is the "now." Everything that happens is in the present moment. Each great decision ever made is made in the grace of the present moment. Every moment we can say 'yes' or 'no' to love and 'yes' or 'no' to God. Adam and Eve, in one moment, changed the history of the world by their one decision to say 'no' to God and 'yes' to Satan. Jesus, in one moment, said 'yes' to the Father, "Not my will but, your will be done" (Matthew 26:39) and, He changed the history of the world.

Mary, in one moment, said 'yes' to the call of God, "Behold the handmaiden of the Lord. Be it done to me according to your word" (Luke 1:38) and, Jesus came to life within her. We can say 'yes' at any present moment and receive the grace of God and conceive of the life of Jesus within us, and start to live the life of Jesus and nourish His life within us.

Each moment of life, we can be like the Good Thief on the cross and turn to Jesus and receive His promise of paradise, if we will live His life and be crucified with Him and accept the cross. Each moment of life is glorious, and we can choose to say, "I will live your life today, I will live in union with you and embrace what you have given me today and embrace my trials and my cross with you for the salvation of the world."

Jesus will say to us, "You have just opened the door for me to come in and give you my very life to live. You are with me in paradise today."

132

It is what it is to be a Christian. A Christian is another Christ. It is to let Jesus live His life in us. "I live, no longer I, but Christ lives within me" (Galatians 2:20).

It could be the sacrament of the present moment because, as in Holy Communion, Jesus wants to come and live His life in us. Each moment and each day, if we allow Him, He will come and live in us. We must embrace the present situation, the 'now.' We must embrace our 'internal now reality' with all of our fears, worries, anxieties, and emotional turmoil and doubts and our 'external now reality' whatever it is, be it sickness, poverty, persecution, or rejection.

For example, you go into the chapel to pray. You can say, "Jesus, I believe you love me right now and that you call me to surrender to your love now, today, right here. I want you to come into my life more deeply, and I want to unite with you now and surrender to you. I want to start again to live your life today. I trust in you to be in me and with me, and I believe that my 'yes' to you allows your Holy Spirit to come into my life and make me another Mary, carrying your life within me. I want to nourish this life today by my prayer and trust and obedience to you, as Mary did. I want to give the life of Jesus to others and the world as Mary did. I believe you are calling me as she was, and that my 'yes' is essential. I believe that you want me to be Jesus in the world. I am sent into the world to be a saviour with and in Jesus. I want to say today, 'yes' to this call."

You can renew this 'yes' every day and many times a day by repentance and prayer, and we can be Jesus as we are called to live. Every time we pray, we pray in Jesus and with Jesus, and we make that act of trust and faith that this very moment has value and power and consequences even as the decision of Jesus and Mary had in their present moment.

The realization of the 'now' moment makes life exciting and vibrant. Each moment is pregnant with meaning and power, as was the very moment that Mary said 'let it be done according to your word.' We must trust that our life is the life of Jesus and that everything we do in union with Jesus is great and helps in the salvation of the world. It is why in the church, we live out the life of Jesus when we unite with Him at Christmas, Lent, Good Friday, Easter, Pentecost. The church lives the life of Jesus. We are called as the church to live the life of Jesus and to redeem the world with, and in Jesus, as we live out His life in the liturgical year. If we live this faith, then life has significant meaning, excitement, and power, for we are most important in the drama of life and can share the work of Jesus and Mary for the salvation of the world.

We can do this every day and every hour, and even if we fail, we can trust in His mercy and keep starting over again. Wow! What a beautiful, exciting life! Please try it! I am praying that you will.

47. HOW CAN YOU DO THE IMPOSSIBLE?

You are commanded by Jesus to love one another as He has loved us!

He also asks us to love Him with "All of our heart and mind and strength" (Mark 12:30). I think that it is impossible for me to do. Can you do it? Have you done it? God does it in us as we surrender. It is impossible apart from Him.

"Divine power has given us everything we need for life and godliness through our knowledge of God, who called us to share in the divine glory and goodness. In bestowing these gifts, God has given us the guarantee of something very great and wonderful to come. Through them you'll be able to share the divine nature." (2 Peter 1:3-4)

There you have it. We are called to participate in the very nature of God, which is love itself. God became man so that man may become God. Man does not become God totally as Jesus is, but he shares by baptism in God's life and become one with Him in His divinity. As we trust in Jesus and surrender to His love, and open our heart to invite Him to come in, and love in us, and give us His love for the Father and others, then everything starts to change. He becomes one with us so that all He does is ours. He does the impossible in us. All He has, becomes ours, for the two become one in a Holy union.

He commands us to love one another as He loves us. It is impossible for us unless He is in us to do this within us. If you decide to let Him be in charge and trust in His mercy and power, then He can do the impossible in us.

Remember, it is God in you that loves God! You, on your own, don't know how to love God. It is Christ in you that recognizes Christ. It is the Holy Spirit, whose temple you are that responds to the Holy Spirit. "Do you not know that you are God's temple and that God's Spirit dwells in you?" (1Corinthians 3:16)

Only so far as you have surrendered to Christ, and allowed the Christ in you to come to fullness, can you love Christ. Give up on relying on your efforts and keep asking the Holy Spirit to come in and give you His power. St. Peter had a profoundly human love for Jesus, but human love is not enough. When fear came in, he denied three times that he even knew Jesus. Peter needed to have divine life; God and the Holy Spirit within him, with His gifts and power. After Peter prayed for nine days with Mary and the apostles, seeking the Holy Spirit, then he had courage and strength.

Do a 9-day novena in preparation for your own Pentecost, asking for a fresh outpouring of the Holy Spirit.

48. PRAYER ANSWERED

"Dear Father Clair, I pray and pray and do not get any help, it seems. Those I pray for even get worse. Can you explain this? It discourages me and erodes my faith."

I pray that my answer helps you. (Let us see if God answers this prayer now.)

My answer: Think. What if you did not pray? Would that make it better? Would the situation not be the same, or perhaps a lot worse? It is a mystery, but I know and trust that even if the external does not seem to change our inner life and our heart changes, and we draw closer to the Lord.

I prayed for over ten years for my parents, and they seemed to get worse and worse, but then there was a significant change beyond my dreams. An incredible conversion, and then the Lord showed me that by my perseverance in prayer, even in the darkness, drew me closer to Jesus and changed my whole life for the good. And then my parents accepted the grace to change too.

One day we will see the power of prayer. But for now, "Blessed are those who have not seen and yet have come to believe." (John 20:29)

Jesus constantly prays at the right hand of the Father for us, but we still have the freedom to choose, and we must say yes to His help, or it will not be able to happen. His prayer gives us the power to change if we choose to and want to change. There is the mystery of our free will. God, in answer to prayer, keeps giving more grace and help to us and to others for whom we pray, but He does not force us to accept the grace. People can refuse God's grace and help.

Statistics seem to indicate that prayer makes a difference. In marriages where they pray together, one in one thousand breaks up, but in marriages in which they do not pray, nearly forty percent break up. My own experience over fifty years as a priest is that all the people who persevere in prayer end up with more peace and joy than those who do not pray. I believe they end up in Heaven.

I find that God answers many, many of my prayers, often in hidden ways that it takes me some thought to see it. Many things He does not seem to answer but, as the years go by, I often perceive the answer. Occasionally there is an obvious, miraculous answer that only He could do. Make a promise and a resolution that you will persevere in prayer no matter how painful or difficult. Do it for God and yourself and for those you love. Try resting in the heart of Jesus, even if only for 3-5 minutes. You will be greatly blessed. He is the source of life and joy and peace, and He loves you with infinite love.

He is knocking, let Him come in. If you cannot find a church that you can visit, make a prayer chapel in your home. Even a table in your bedroom with a crucifix, a picture of Jesus, and a Bible makes a little altar for the Lord. Why not? I pray in faith that this helps. Remember also, if prayer is not answered in this world, it is in the next for all of the good desires of our heart are fulfilled in Heaven!

49. PRICELESS DIAMONDS

God is like the father of the prodigal son, foolishly loving, forgetting that the son squandered his money and ruined everything, and lived his own selfish life.

Each moment of life is like precious diamonds. But they look a little black and grubby. A little bit like if you had a rich father and he was going to leave. He said, "I am going to leave, but I'm going to give you a special gift." He hands you a bucket. "Goodbye, don't forget the gift, son."

You look in the bucket, and there's a whole bunch of dirty stones. You think, "What? Why would my father give me a bucket with a bunch of black stones? Strange. I don't know what to do."

Then you throw the black stones away. Maybe as a kid, you shoot them from a slingshot or play with them. Put some in the gravel on the driveway. Don't pay attention to them very much. Then one day, a person comes in, and they look at the few black stones left in your bucket and say, "Did you realize those are priceless diamonds? If you take that to a jeweler, they will give you a lot of money for them."

"But I threw most of them away! I'm 81 years old now. How am I going to have money for retirement?"

"Well, you've still got a lot of diamonds left since they are still covering the bottom of the bucket. They are so precious."

I still have a few moments of 1 may even have three or four years left, and every moment of my life is that precious diamond, that precious gift from God if I'll embrace it and live that moment for Him. It's exciting. I can make up for my past, where I wasted so much time and didn't realize the value of each moment of my life. So I like to stop frequently and give you glory, God; Glory to the Father and to the Son and to the Holy Spirit.

That's why I find this an incredible secret because then I can never get discouraged. Every day is a whole new life, a whole new chance to live for God. In the morning, I like to get up and say, "Today is a whole new life. The past is gone. I get to live for God today. There is a tremendous reward for every moment of this day. I offer it to You. Lord, I offer You all my prayers. I offer You my work. I offer You my sufferings, my joys, my sorrows. At this moment, I offer it all to You. I'm going to keep offering it to You all through the day. I give You glory all through the day. Because I believe every moment of life You planned was a gift and a reward. And every moment of life, I can grow in holiness if I choose the good and offer that moment to You. Every moment of life You have a special grace because You love me. Each moment is pregnant with a gift like a jewel."

Why do I believe this? Why would I think this? God loves me more than I would love my child, if I was a father and had a child.

I know in my heart, if I had a child and I had all power, I would plan that child's life so that every moment of his life led him to more capacity for the happiness I have planned for him. I would want that child to grow in capacity for joy every hour of this life so that he could come to complete happiness because I desire complete happiness for the people I love. And if I want that and I am a selfish person, how much more does God want complete happiness for every one of us because He created us for joy, to be with Him? I make that act of faith.

Each moment of my life is pregnant with life and meaning. God has a plan to lead me to perfect, glorious happiness that I can't even imagine. So I am going to try to embrace and receive the gift God has for me and not waste a moment of my life.

50. MESSAGE OF CHRISTMAS

Are you giving those you love a gift at Christmas?

Are you at least praying for those you love, and perhaps phoning them or writing them? It is Jesus's birthday! What are you giving him for his birthday? God is giving you his whole self and eternal riches in Heaven and victory over death. Are you grateful, and are you thanking him for his gift? If someone gave you a million dollars, you would be rejoicing and celebrating and thanking the person. Jesus is asking you for a gift, for it is his birthday. What gift does Jesus want from you?

He wants your love and your gift of yourself! He gave his whole self to you and continues to give himself to you in Holy Communion. I am praying for you that you will have great joy in God's Christmas gift to you and that you will give Jesus the Christmas present that He wants from you.

All life comes from a love relationship--indeed all existence. It is because God is a love relationship between three persons; the Father, the Son, and the Holy Spirit. God is love, the scripture says. He is a raging fire of love, and His love explodes into the creation of the universe. The fire of the sun and the stars is an image of the fire of God's love.

"God so loved the world that He gave his only Son so that whoever believes in Him may have everlasting life." (John 3:16) Jesus is the incarnation of God's love for us. The universe is a sign of the greatness of His love for us as human beings. Love forms a bond between two persons who love each other. If the love is mutual, the two are bonded together, and they become one. In marriage, they become one flesh. Jesus became one with us in our human flesh on Christmas day.

Sin is a disease that destroys the love bond between persons. Joy comes when people genuinely love God and one another. Imagine, if we all loved God and each other, there would be no more war or hatred or rape or murder or divorce or starvation or poverty, because we would all care for each other and have loving compassion for each other.

At this time, when God came into our world to restore love and union with God and each other and to redeem the world from sin, let us look at our love bonds with God and each other. Are we in a love relationship with God in Jesus and with each other? Love bonds between persons take time to build. We must make time to be together. You cannot be deeply bonded in union with anyone if you are too lazy or too much in love with yourself to create time to be with the one you choose to love. Marriages and deep love relationships fall apart when there are little communication and real love.

If there was a big birthday celebration for our friend or our father or our spouse and we did not make time to spend the day and be there with them, could we say we have an important love relationship with them? How is your love bond going with God in Jesus? Do you make time to commune with your God and your saviour Jesus? Have you built a deep, strong love bond with the one who gave you life and died on the cross to save you? Will you set aside time to be with Jesus on His birthday celebration this Christmas?

Many of the Saints tell us that getting to Heaven is very simple. If you make time for sincere and genuine prayer communion and build the love bond with Jesus, you will rise with Him from the dead and be with Him in a union in His glory because you lived in union with Him on earth. If you do not live in union with Him on earth and do not seek Him in prayer, then you cannot be in union with Him when you die, nor can you ascend to Heaven with Him.

Ask God for the gift of prayer. Build a love bond with Jesus by making time for Him in prayer. Jesus became a human being to unite with you in love, so you cold unite with Him and share His life and happiness in Heaven.

51. A GOD SIZE HOLE

Just as our body hungers for food, so our soul hungers for love and happiness.

Everything we do is to fill the emptiness inside of us. Our bodily hunger for food is a sign of all the other deep hungers. How do people try to fill that emptiness? They try many, many different things. Our soul and mind and heart hunger for as many things as your body does for all the many kinds of food. But all the things that we seek are to fill our emptiness and to make us happier and more fulfilled. Everything we seek is a tiny reflection of God and a little bit of His goodness, but God alone can fill our emptiness, for our heart was made for Him and has a God-sized hole in it only he can fill.

What do you seek to make you feel more fulfilled, satisfied, and happy? I have in the past filled myself and my time with eating, watching TV, talking to friends, sports, hobbies, work, reading, study, etc. I have got captured by such things as travel, mountain climbing, hiking, riding horses, playing chess, love relationships, and prayer. I've tried almost everything to fill up my life and my emptiness, and make me a little happier and content.

I found that the most satisfying and powerful things that have filled my emptiness are my love relationships with God and with others. I have been captured and even addicted to things that have left me empty in the end. They have blotted out to a degree, the more critical things such as love of God and others. Some of the things that have captured me are opposed to real love and have only fostered a love of self.

What about you? What have you spent your time seeking? Have the things of the world given you peace and happiness? Have they captured so much of your time and heart that you have neglected prayer and growing in holiness and love of God? Are you willing to let go of some of the things that you are captured by and that you spend your time seeking? Do you want to change? Are you willing to ask God to help you put Him first and to let go of some of the things you spend your time on?

For me, it was at times, life, or death forever because some things had captured me that could have gradually led me almost entirely away from God. Remember, the whole purpose of our life is to grow in the love of God and others so that we are prepared for the end of our journey and are ready and capable of life in Heaven.

Psalm 62 tells us that in God alone is my soul at rest. This psalm goes on to say to us to trust in Him at all times, and to pour out our heart before Him for in God alone is our complete happiness. Lord, gather us under the shadow of your wings and keep us as the apple of your eye!

52. GOING FOR THE FINISH LINE

My journey of life is nearing the end, and so I'm going all out for the finish line.

Saint Paul in Philippians 3:12-14 perfectly expresses what I feel in my heart. "Not that I have already obtained this or have already reached the goal, but I press on to make it my own because Christ Jesus has made me his own. Beloved, I do not consider that I have made it my own; but this one thing I do: forgetting what lies behind and straining forward to what lies ahead, I press on towards the goal for the prize of the heavenly call of God in Christ Jesus."

I have not quite reached the end of my life as yet, but I want to go all out, heading for the reward that God has prepared for me in His mercy and love. Since I've let Jesus grasp me and come into my life more fully, I see the truth as Saint Paul did. I do not want to look at the past anymore, or my failures. I want to give my undivided attention to the finish line to which God is calling me, and which is life in Heaven with Jesus and all the saints.

I feel weak and sick and that I can't go on, and a little discouraged at times. However, as I pray and turn to Jesus, He renews me and gives me new strength. In His love and mercy, He helps me not to quit, but to continue to run and even run faster than I have before.

I see that the finish line is close at hand, and the only important thing is to grow in love and prayer and seek Him with all my heart and all my strength. Jesus helps me to resist the temptation to take it easy and not to run very much, not to make that effort to pray when it's difficult. It is a strong temptation, sometimes when you're old and not feeling very well. I pray to the Sacred Heart of Jesus that I could let go of the past, both the good and the bad, and give it over to him and trust in His love and mercy.

With His help, I trust in Jesus to repair what is broken and restore what is lost and heal what is wounded, and right what is wrong. Jesus will transform every evil to good by His Redeeming Grace.

I ask all of you to pray this prayer with me over and over again:

"Jesus hold onto me and never let me go,
so that my entire attention is on the finish line,
and you are calling me to life in Heaven with You,
Lord.
Jesus, You are my prize, and my hope, and my reward.
I can do all things in You who strengthen me."

I try to do always what the Lord wants me all to do. It is His message to you and me in sacred scripture, "For those who live according to the Spirit set their minds on the things of the Spirit. To set the mind on the flesh is death, but to set the mind on the Spirit is life and peace."
(Romans 8:5-7).
It could be my final message. It is undoubtedly the most important thing of all in my life and everyone's life. God bless you always.

Author

Father Clair Watrin, CSB, has served in many roles, including parish work, secondary and postsecondary teaching and 15 years as a missionary in Saint Lucia. He is the founder of the Live-In Retreat movement, helped establish Catholic Christian Outreach at the University of Saskatchewan, and served as the chaplain at the Way of Holiness Retreat Center in Hinton. He is now retired and living at the Cardinal Flahiff Basilian Centre in Toronto.

Editor

Alice Murray has a degree in Communication and has spent 30 years working in the oil and gas industry in community involvement. She is now retired and divides her time between writing, sewing, farming, Live-Ins, and her seven adorable grandchildren.

Acknowledgments

First I would like to thank Father Clair for his insight, humour, and grace in writing these words of meditation and inspiration and for entrusting them to me in the creation of this book. It is our greatest wish that these words glorify God and bring a glimpse of His joy and peace to those who read it.

We would also like to thank Pat Tempro for her work in sharing Father Clair's blog out to the world.

To the Live-In Community whose love for Father Clair was the motivation for this book.

I personally would like to thank Wanda Landis and Bernie Visotto, my writing buddies who continued to cheer me on to get this project over the finish line.

To Simon Appolloni, editorial director of Novalis Publishing for his feedback and suggestions to make this a better book.

And last but certainly not least, to my family. You help me, inspire me, and show me what God's love looks like every day.

Made in the USA
San Bernardino, CA
19 May 2020

71260886R00100